THREADS OF UNITY
WEAVING HAITI'S NEW DAWN

BY

SABAT BEATTO

COPYRIGHT

Copyright © 2024 by Sabat Beatto

This book is a work of fiction. The information and advice provided are based on the author's research, knowledge, and personal experiences. Any references to specific individuals, organizations, or events are intended for illustrative purposes and do not imply endorsement or affiliation.

The views and opinions expressed in this book are those of the author and do not necessarily reflect the official policy or position of any person or organization mentioned.

TABLE OF CONTENTS

INTRODUCTION 5

CHAPTER 1 : ANNETTE'S DESCHAMPS 7

CHAPTER 2 : MARCUS TURNER 10

CHAPTER 3 : PROFESSOR SOPHIE MOREAU 13

CHAPTER 4 : JEAN-CLAUDE DESMARAIS 16

CHAPTER 5 : SHEIKH AHMED AL-FARSI 18

CHAPTER 6 : BISHOP ESPERANZA RUIZ 20

CHAPTER 7 : RABBI MIRIAM COHEN 22

CHAPTER 8 : PRESIDENT MARTINE LAURENT 25

CHAPTER 9 : A GATHERING OF MINDS 29

CHAPTER 10 : THE HISTORY OF HAITI 32

CHAPTER 11 : CONNECTING WITH THE HEART OF HAITI.....34

CHAPTER 12 : SHADOWS WITHIN 37

CHAPTER 13 : RESOLVING INNER TURMOIL...........................39

CHAPTER 14 : SHADOWS OF DESPAIR 42

CHAPTER 15 : CONVERGENCE OF MINDS 44

CHAPTER 16 : THE CHALLENGE OF INTERNATIONAL COLLABORATION46

CHAPTER 17 : FORGING UNITY..51

CHAPTER 18 : WHISPERS IN THE SHADOWS 54

CHAPTER 19 : THREADS OF HOPE...57

CHAPTER 20 : ECONOMIC RESURGENCE................................60

CHAPTER 21 : STREETS OF DETERMINATION 66

CHAPTER 22 : SISTER MARIE'S SCHOOL OF DREAMS 70

CHAPTER 23 : JEAN-CLAUDE'S BLUEPRINT 74

CHAPTER 24 : INVESTING IN TOMORROW 78

CHAPTER 25 : BUILDING BRIDGES 81

CHAPTER 26 : ANNETTE'S VISION: BEYOND THE TURMOIL 85

CHAPTER 27 : RAYS OF EDUCATION 89

CHAPTER 28 : THE MOSQUE ON ELM STREET 93

CHAPTER 29 : UNRAVELING DISASTER 98

CHAPTER 30 : HARMONY AMIDST CHAOS 101

CHAPTER 31 : RESILIENCE IN THE RUINS 106

CHAPTER 32 : MARCUS'S INVESTMENTS: SEEDS OF CHANGE 111

CHAPTER 33 : HAITI'S RISING 117

CHAPTER 34 : SOWING PROSPERITY 122

CHAPTER 35 : RISING FROM ASHES 127

CHAPTER 36 : TEMPLE OF TRANSFORMATION 131

CHAPTER 37 : HOPE IN THE HOTEL INDUSTRY 135

CHAPTER 38 : ANNETTE'S WAR ON POVERTY 139

CHAPTER 39 : JEAN-CLAUDE'S REVOLUTION 142

CHAPTER 40 : SCHOOLING THE STREETS 147

CHAPTER 41 : BISHOP RUIZ'S SERMON OF UNITY 154

CHAPTER 42 : HAITI'S SYMPHONY 159

CHAPTER 43 : A NEW DAWN FOR HAITI 163

CHAPTER 44 : BREAKING CHAINS 167

CHAPTER 45 : EMBRACING PEACE 171

CHAPTER 46 : THE PROMISED LAND 173

INTRODUCTION

In the heart of a nation grappling with the tides of change, a chorus of diverse voices rises above the din of challenges. These are the voices of leaders, each carrying a torch of hope that flickers brightly against the backdrop of Haiti's struggles. Here, where shadows dance, and despair threatens to extinguish the spirit of the people, these leaders stand united, their unwavering resolve a beacon of change.

But before we unravel the complex tapestry of Haiti's history, a journey etched with trials that have shaped its destiny, let us pause and turn our attention to the individuals at the forefront of this transformative odyssey. In the forthcoming chapters, we will embark on a captivating exploration, delving into the intricate details of their lives. We will uncover the stories that lie beneath the surface, exploring their backgrounds, the essence of their motivations, and the battles that have sculpted them into the pillars of resilience and unwavering determination they are today.

From Bishop Ruiz, whose unwavering commitment to social justice burns with an inextinguishable flame, to Annette, whose tireless advocacy for unity and education echoes throughout the land, each character brings a unique perspective and an unyielding strength to the table.

Join us as we embark on a captivating voyage that traverses the corridors of power, plumbs the depths of human resilience, and unveils the intricate dance of collaboration, all while the story of Haiti's tumultuous past paints a vivid backdrop.

Together, let us embark on a quest to untangle the threads that bind these characters and their nation, weaving a tapestry rich with narratives of hope, courage, and the enduring spirit that defines the Haitian people.

CHAPTER 1
ANNETTE'S DESCHAMPS

In the heart of Port-au-Prince, where the streets echoed with the rhythms of life, Annette's journey began. Born into a family of humble origins, Annette's childhood was steeped in the vibrant tapestry of Haiti's culture and traditions. From an early age, she was captivated by the spirit of unity that defined her community, where people from all walks of life came together to celebrate their shared humanity.

Annette's parents, hardworking and devoted to their community, instilled in her a deep sense of compassion and a belief in the power of unity to overcome adversity. They taught her that no matter how daunting the challenges may seem, there is always hope to be found in the bonds that unite us.

Annette stood at the edge of the busy marketplace in Port-au-Prince. She watched life unfold before her, with colorful scenes all around. Vendors haggled, children laughed, and music played, creating a lively atmosphere. Amidst the energy, Annette felt a strong sense of purpose.

As she grew older, Annette became increasingly aware of the inequalities that plagued her country. She witnessed firsthand the struggles of her neighbors – families grappling with poverty, children denied access to education, and communities torn apart by violence. It was a stark reminder of the injustices that persisted in Haiti, despite its rich cultural heritage and resilient spirit.

But amidst the challenges, Annette found inspiration in the stories of courage and hope that echoed through the streets. She saw the tireless efforts of community leaders who worked tirelessly to uplift their neighbors, the resilience of families who found joy in the simplest moments, and the unwavering spirit of the Haitian people who refused to be defined by their circumstances.

 Motivated by a desire to make a difference, Annette embarked on a journey of self-discovery and activism. She immersed herself in community organizing efforts, mobilizing her peers to address pressing issues such as access to education, economic empowerment, and social justice. Through her tireless advocacy, Annette emerged as a beacon of hope for those who had long been marginalized and overlooked.

But Annette's path was not without its challenges. As a young woman navigating the complexities of Haitian society, she encountered skepticism and resistance from those who doubted her ability to effect meaningful change. She faced criticism for her unconventional approach to community development, with some dismissing her efforts as naive or idealistic.

Undeterred by the naysayers, Annette pressed on, fueled by her unwavering belief in the transformative power of unity and hope. She understood that real change would only come through collective action – by bringing people together, regardless of their differences, to work towards a common goal. It was this vision that inspired her to launch the Threads of Hope initiative, a grassroots movement aimed at weaving together the diverse threads of Haiti's community to create a tapestry of resilience and strength.

Through Threads of Hope, Annette sought to integrate unity into every aspect of the community's transformation. She worked tirelessly to promote education, economic empowerment, and community engagement, recognizing that these were the building blocks of a brighter future for Haiti. Whether it was organizing vocational training programs for at-risk youth, supporting local businesses through microfinance initiatives, or fostering dialogue among religious and cultural groups, Annette's efforts were guided by a commitment to uplifting her community from within.

But the road ahead was fraught with challenges. Annette faced opposition from entrenched interests resistant to change, as well as the ever-present threat of violence from criminal gangs that sought to maintain their grip on power. Yet through it all, she remained steadfast in her conviction that hope could triumph over despair – that by weaving together the threads of unity, the people of Haiti could overcome even the greatest of obstacles.

As Annette stood on the streets of Port-au-Prince, surrounded by the vibrant tapestry of her community, she knew that the journey towards a brighter future was far from over. But with the Threads of Hope guiding their way, she was confident that together, they could overcome any challenge and build a Haiti where unity, resilience, and hope reigned supreme.

And so, the story of Annette's journey continued, a testament to the indomitable spirit of the Haitian people and the power of one woman's determination to make a difference in the world.

CHAPTER 2
MARCUS TURNER

Marcus stood at the edge of the bustling marketplace, his gaze scanning the vibrant scene before him. The air was filled with sounds. Vendors were selling their goods. Shoppers were talking about prices. Carts carrying fresh produce were making noise. It was a familiar sight, one that reminded Marcus of his humble beginnings and the journey that had led him to this moment.

Born into a working-class family in the heart of Port-au-Prince, Marcus grew up surrounded by the sights and sounds of the marketplace. His parents, small-scale entrepreneurs who ran a modest grocery stall, instilled in him a strong work ethic and a deep appreciation for the value of economic independence. From a young age, Marcus understood the pivotal role that economic empowerment played in shaping the trajectory of one's life.

Motivated by a desire to uplift his community and create opportunities for those who had been left behind, Marcus embarked on a journey of self-discovery and entrepreneurship. He immersed himself in the world of business, honing his skills as a strategic thinker and visionary leader. With each success and setback, Marcus learned valuable lessons. He learned about the details of economic growth and development.

But Marcus's path was not without its struggles. As a young entrepreneur navigating the complex landscape of Haiti's economy, he encountered numerous challenges along the way.

Bureaucratic red tape and corruption were major problems. So were limited access to capital and resources. Marcus faced these obstacles at every turn. Yet, it was precisely these challenges that fueled his determination to effect meaningful change.

He had a deep belief in the power of economic empowerment. This led Marcus to become a vocal advocate for investing in local businesses. This meant creating jobs and sustainable economic policies. He understood that poverty and inequality were not just moral issues but also impediments to overall community growth and prosperity. Through his tireless advocacy, Marcus sought to address these systemic barriers and pave the way for a brighter future for Haiti.

One of Marcus's proudest achievements was his role in spearheading initiatives to support local entrepreneurs and promote economic resilience. Marcus was instrumental in empowering his fellow Haitians to chart their own paths to success. He did this through microfinance programs. They provided small loans to budding business owners. He also ran vocational training initiatives. These gave people the skills needed to thrive in a competitive market.

But the road ahead was fraught with challenges. Marcus faced resistance from entrenched interests. They were resistant to change. He also faced the ever-present specter of economic instability that loomed over Haiti. Yet, through it all, he remained steadfast in his conviction that sustainable economic development was the key to unlocking the nation's full potential.

As Marcus looked out over the bustling marketplace, he felt a sense of pride in how far he had come and a renewed determination to continue his quest for economic empowerment. He knew that the seeds of prosperity had been planted.

With dedication, perseverance, and strategic thinking, he was confident that they would flourish, transforming Haiti into a land of opportunity for all who called it home.

CHAPTER 3
PROFESSOR SOPHIE MOREAU

Professor Sophie stood before her classroom. She was a beacon of knowledge and inspiration in the busy city of Port-au-Prince. With a passion for education burning brightly within her, she embarked on a journey that would shape the lives of countless young minds and ignite a flame of hope in the hearts of her students.

Born into a family of intellectuals in the historic city of Jacmel, Sophie's childhood was steeped in books, discussions, and a deep appreciation for learning. Her parents, both renowned scholars in their respective fields, instilled in her a love for knowledge and a thirst for understanding the world around her.

From an early age, Sophie displayed a remarkable aptitude for academics, devouring books and absorbing information with a voracious appetite. She excelled in school, earning top marks and garnering praise from her teachers for her insightful analysis and critical thinking skills.

Sophie was motivated by a deep sense of purpose and a desire to level the playing field for all children. She dedicated herself to championing educational reform. She knew education wasn't just for knowledge. It was also a tool for driving change and empowering youth to reach their full potential.

Sophie's journey was not without its struggles. She navigated Haiti's bureaucratic education system and faced resistance from entrenched interests that did not want change.

Budget constraints, overcrowded classrooms, and a lack of resources posed formidable obstacles to her vision of quality education accessible to all.

Undeterred by the challenges she faced, Sophie forged ahead, leveraging her position as a respected educator to push for meaningful reforms. She advocated for increased funding for schools in underserved communities, lobbied for policies that promoted equal access to education, and spearheaded initiatives to improve teacher training and curriculum development.

But Sophie's efforts went beyond the confines of the classroom. She understood the importance of community engagement in driving educational reform and worked tirelessly to build partnerships with parents, community leaders, and policymakers. Through town hall meetings, grassroots campaigns, and advocacy work, she rallied support for her vision of a more equitable education system.

One of Sophie's most significant achievements was her role in establishing community learning centers in marginalized neighborhoods. These centers served as hubs of educational excellence, providing children with access to quality instruction, mentorship programs, and extracurricular activities that enriched their lives and expanded their horizons.

As Sophie looked out over her classroom, filled with eager young minds hungry for knowledge, she felt a sense of fulfillment, knowing that she was making a difference in the lives of her students. Despite the challenges she faced along the way, she remained unwavering in her commitment to providing every child in Haiti with the opportunity to receive a quality education.

For Sophie, education was more than just a profession—it was a calling, a lifelong mission to illuminate the path to a brighter future for the youth of Haiti. And as she continued her journey, she did so with the unwavering belief that knowledge was the key to unlocking the potential of her beloved country and shaping a better tomorrow for generations to come.

CHAPTER 4
JEAN-CLAUDE DESMARAIS

Jean-Claude's journey as an economist began long before he stepped into the busy streets of Port-au-Prince. Born into a family of modest means, he learned the value of hard work and perseverance from an early age. Growing up in a neighborhood where economic opportunities were scarce, Jean-Claude witnessed the struggles of his community firsthand and felt a deep-seated desire to make a difference.

Driven by a passion for economics and a commitment to uplifting his fellow Haitians, Jean-Claude pursued higher education, earning degrees in economics and business administration. Armed with knowledge and determination, he embarked on a career focused on economic empowerment and community development.

As a seasoned economist, Jean-Claude understood the critical role that inclusive economic policies played in fostering community prosperity. He believed that sustainable economic growth could only be achieved by empowering all members of society, especially those from marginalized backgrounds.

Jean-Claude's advocacy for inclusive economic policies extended to his work with local businesses and entrepreneurs. He recognized the potential for small businesses to serve as engines of growth and job creation in Haiti's economy and advocated for policies that supported their development.

From microfinance initiatives to support for local cooperatives, Jean-Claude championed programs that provided access to capital and resources for aspiring entrepreneurs.

Despite his passion for economic empowerment, Jean-Claude faced numerous challenges along the way. Limited resources, bureaucratic red tape, and entrenched interests posed formidable obstacles to his efforts to implement meaningful change. Yet, he remained undeterred, leveraging his expertise and influence to navigate the complexities of Haiti's economic landscape.

One of Jean-Claude's proudest achievements was his role in the establishment of vocational training programs in underserved communities. These programs provided individuals with the skills and knowledge needed to access employment opportunities and contribute to the local economy. Through hands-on training and mentorship, Jean-Claude helped empower countless individuals to build better futures for themselves and their families.

As Jean-Claude looked back on his journey, he saw the impact of his work reflected in the faces of the people he had helped empower. From budding entrepreneurs launching their businesses to skilled workers finding meaningful employment, he knew that his efforts had made a tangible difference in the lives of his fellow Haitians.

For Jean-Claude, the pursuit of economic empowerment was not just a professional endeavor—it was a personal mission rooted in his deep love for his country and its people. And as he continued on his journey, he did so with a renewed sense of purpose, knowing that every step he took brought Haiti one step closer to a future of prosperity and opportunity for all.

CHAPTER 5
SHEIKH AHMED AL-FARSI

Sheikh Ahmed's journey as a leader within the Islamic community was shaped by a deep sense of faith and a commitment to promoting unity and understanding among people of all faiths. Born into a devout family, Sheikh Ahmed was raised with a strong sense of Islamic values and teachings, instilling in him a deep respect for diversity and a belief in the power of unity.

Growing up in a community where people of different faiths coexisted harmoniously, Sheikh Ahmed witnessed firsthand the beauty that emerged when people came together in solidarity, regardless of their religious beliefs. Inspired by this spirit of inclusivity, he dedicated himself to fostering interfaith collaboration and celebrating the rich diversity that defined his community.

As a young leader within the Islamic community, Sheikh Ahmed faced the challenge of navigating tensions and misunderstandings that sometimes arose between different religious groups. Yet, he remained steadfast in his belief that dialogue, understanding, and cooperation were the keys to overcoming these challenges and building a more inclusive society.

Sheikh Ahmed's advocacy for interfaith collaboration extended beyond mere words—it was a core principle that guided his actions and interactions with others.

He actively sought out opportunities to engage with leaders and members of other faith communities, fostering meaningful relationships built on mutual respect and understanding.

One of Sheikh Ahmed's most significant contributions was his role in organizing interfaith events and initiatives aimed at promoting dialogue and cooperation among people of different faiths. These events provided platforms for individuals to come together, share their stories, and learn from one another, fostering a sense of solidarity and empathy that transcended religious boundaries.

Despite his unwavering commitment to promoting unity and inclusivity, Sheikh Ahmed faced challenges along the way. Skepticism, prejudice, and resistance from some quarters tested his resolve, but he remained undeterred, drawing strength from his faith and the support of like-minded individuals who shared his vision for a more harmonious world.

For Sheikh Ahmed, the journey towards unity was not just a matter of religious doctrine—it was a deeply personal mission rooted in his belief in the inherent dignity and worth of every human being. And as he continued on his journey, he did so with a sense of hope and optimism, knowing that by working together, people of all faiths could create a world where diversity was celebrated, and unity prevailed.

CHAPTER 6
BISHOP ESPERANZA RUIZ

Amidst the hustle and bustle of everyday life, a small church stood as a sanctuary amid towering skyscrapers and busy streets. This quiet haven, tucked away in the shadows of the urban jungle, marked the starting point of Bishop Ruiz's journey.

Born into a family of modest means, Bishop Ruiz spent his childhood in the vibrant streets of his neighborhood. From a young age, he was drawn to the teachings of the Catholic Church, finding solace and inspiration in its message of compassion, justice, and forgiveness.

As Bishop Ruiz grew older, he witnessed firsthand the deep-rooted inequities and injustices that plagued his community. He saw families struggling to make ends meet, children living in poverty, and marginalized communities being pushed to the fringes of society.

But amidst the darkness, Bishop Ruiz saw a glimmer of hope – a belief that with compassion and understanding, change was possible. Inspired by the teachings of Jesus Christ, who preached love and compassion for all, Bishop Ruiz dedicated his life to advocating for the marginalized and the oppressed.

Driven by his faith and guided by his principles, Bishop Ruiz became a voice for the voiceless, speaking out against injustice and standing up for those who had been silenced by society.

He worked tirelessly to address the root causes of poverty and inequality, advocating for policies that would uplift the most vulnerable members of society.

But Bishop Ruiz's journey was not without its struggles. He faced opposition from those who sought to maintain the status quo and protect their own interests. He faced questioning and doubt from people questioning whether his idea for a fairer and kinder society could work.

Undeterred by the challenges he faced, Bishop Ruiz remained steadfast in his commitment to his faith and his calling to serve the most vulnerable members of society. He continued to be a beacon of hope and inspiration in his community, leading by example and demonstrating the transformative power of compassion and empathy.

And so, as Bishop Ruiz stood at the pulpit of his small church, surrounded by the faithful who had gathered to hear his message, he knew that his journey was far from over. He was a shepherd of souls, a guardian of justice, and a voice for the voiceless – and he would continue to walk his path with humility, grace, and unwavering faith.

CHAPTER 7
RABBI MIRIAM COHEN

Surrounded by the interwoven sounds of diverse cultures, Rabbi Cohen's journey unfolded. Born into a family with a rich cultural heritage, his childhood was steeped in tradition and history.

Growing up in a close-knit community, Rabbi Cohen was surrounded by the sights, sounds, and smells of his Jewish heritage. From the melodies of Hebrew prayers echoing through the synagogue to the aroma of freshly baked challah bread wafting from his grandmother's kitchen, every aspect of Rabbi Cohen's upbringing was infused with a deep sense of cultural pride and identity.

But amidst the warmth of tradition, Rabbi Cohen also felt a profound sense of responsibility to preserve and celebrate his cultural heritage in a world that was becoming increasingly diverse and interconnected. He recognized that in order to build a truly harmonious society, it was essential to embrace and appreciate the cultural richness of all communities.

Driven by his passion for cultural harmony, Rabbi Cohen dedicated himself to promoting intercultural understanding and appreciation. He worked tirelessly to bridge the gaps between different communities, fostering dialogue and collaboration among people of diverse backgrounds.

One day, during a community gathering, Rabbi Cohen overheard murmurs of discontent among some members of his congregation. Approaching them with a warm smile, he initiated a conversation.

"Is something troubling you, my friends?" Rabbi Cohen inquired, his voice gentle yet firm.

One of the congregants, a middle-aged man, spoke up hesitantly. "Rabbi, I'm concerned about the changes happening around us. Our community has always been tightly knit, but now it feels like we're losing our traditions in the face of all this diversity."

Rabbi Cohen listened attentively, acknowledging the man's concerns. "I understand your apprehensions," he said, his voice reassuring. "But diversity doesn't diminish our traditions – it enriches them. By embracing different cultures, we can learn from one another and strengthen our own identity."

Another congregant, a young woman, spoke up next. "But Rabbi, what if our traditions clash with those of others? How do we navigate that?"

Rabbi Cohen nodded thoughtfully. "It's natural for differences to arise, but how we approach them matters. We can find common ground through respectful dialogue and mutual understanding. Our traditions may vary, but our shared values of compassion and kindness can guide us."

Undeterred by the challenges he faced, Rabbi Cohen remained steadfast in his commitment to promoting cultural harmony and integration. He saw the beauty in diversity and believed that by celebrating and preserving each other's cultural heritage, communities could find strength in their shared humanity.

And so, as Rabbi Cohen stood before his congregation, his voice filled with passion and conviction, he spoke of the importance of cultural harmony. He urged his community to embrace their cultural heritage with pride and to reach out to others with empathy and understanding.

For Rabbi Cohen, cultural harmony was not just a lofty ideal but a guiding principle that shaped his life and work. And as he looked out at the faces of his congregation, he knew that his journey was far from over. He was a guardian of tradition. He championed diversity and cultural harmony. He would continue to walk his path with unwavering dedication and commitment.

CHAPTER 8
PRESIDENT MARTINE LAURENT

In the corridors of power, where decisions shape the destiny of nations, President Martine Laurent's journey began. Born into a family of humble origins, Martine's childhood was marked by the hardships and struggles that defined life for many in her community. Growing up in a neighborhood where poverty cast a long shadow, Martine learned early on the value of resilience and determination.

From a young age, Martine exhibited a natural aptitude for leadership. Whether organizing her peers for community clean-up efforts or rallying support for local initiatives, Martine demonstrated an innate ability to inspire others and effect positive change. Her charisma and passion for making a difference set her apart, earning her the respect and admiration of those around her.

But Martine's path to leadership was not without its challenges. As a woman in a male-dominated society, she faced skepticism and discrimination from those who doubted her ability to lead. Despite the obstacles in her way, Martine refused to be deterred. She knew that her vision for a better future transcended gender barriers, and she was determined to prove herself worthy of the trust placed in her.

Driven by a deep sense of duty to her community, Martine dedicated herself to public service.

She pursued higher education, earning degrees in law and political science, and immersed herself in the intricacies of governance and policy-making. Through hard work and perseverance, Martine rose through the ranks, eventually emerging as a beacon of hope for her people.

As President, Martine faced the formidable task of steering her country through turbulent times. She inherited a nation plagued by economic instability, social unrest, and political turmoil. But Martine refused to succumb to despair. She saw in her country's challenges an opportunity to effect meaningful change – to build a Haiti where every citizen could aspire to a life of dignity, opportunity, and fulfillment.

President Martine Laurent engaged with her community, addressing their concerns and listening to their voices amidst the challenges facing their nation.

One humid afternoon, Martine held an impromptu gathering in a local market, surrounded by vendors and residents eager to share their experiences. A middle-aged woman, clutching her worn-out purse tightly, approached Martine with a furrowed brow.

"Madam President," she began, her voice tinged with worry, "our small businesses are struggling to survive. The economic instability makes it hard to make ends meet. What can we do?"

Martine's gaze softened as she nodded empathetically. "I understand your concerns," she replied, her voice carrying a reassuring tone. "Rest assured, my administration is working to implement measures that will stimulate economic growth and provide support for small businesses like yours. Together, we will overcome these challenges."

As the sun began to set, Martine engaged in another conversation, this time with a group of young students gathered outside a makeshift classroom.

"President Laurent," one of the students spoke up, her eyes filled with determination, "we dream of a Haiti where every child has access to quality education. How can we make this dream a reality?"

Martine's face lit up with passion as she addressed the students. "Education is the cornerstone of a prosperous nation," she declared. "My administration is committed to expanding access to quality education for all children. By investing in our schools, empowering our teachers, and fostering a culture of lifelong learning, we can ensure that every child in Haiti has the opportunity to fulfill their potential."

Through these dialogues and interactions with her community, Martine tackled the pressing issues facing her nation, addressing their concerns with empathy and determination.

Martine's leadership style was defined by her unwavering commitment to the people she served. She listened to their concerns, empathized with their struggles, and sought their input in shaping policies that would impact their lives. She believed in transparency and accountability and worked to root out corruption and inefficiency wherever it was found.

But Martine's greatest challenge came in the form of entrenched criminal gangs that held her country captive. With escalating violence and lawlessness, Martine knew decisive action was needed to confront this threat. She rallied international support, mobilized law enforcement agencies, and implemented bold strategies to dismantle the criminal networks that terrorized her people.

Throughout her journey, Martine remained guided by her unwavering faith in the resilience and potential of her nation. She believed in the power of unity, the promise of progress, and the possibility of a brighter future for Haiti. As she stood at the helm of her country, leading her people toward a new dawn, Martine Laurent embodied the true essence of leadership – courage, compassion, and unwavering dedication to the greater good.

CHAPTER 9
A GATHERING OF MINDS

The sun hung low over the Caribbean horizon, casting a warm glow that filtered through the grand windows of a conference room where destiny awaited. Diverse leaders from both local and international areas gathered at a colossal table. The table mirrored the weight of responsibility they bore. The air crackled with a palpable sense of urgency and hope, their mission clear – to elevate Haiti from the depths of its challenges.

Around the table, a symphony of perspectives unfolded. Representing the heart and soul of Haiti, President Martine Laurent exuded charisma and determination. Her eyes, a reflection of the struggles and resilience of her people, scanned the room with unwavering resolve. Seated beside her, Jean-Claude Desmarais, a luminary economist celebrated for innovative approaches to development, poised his pen over a notebook, ready to translate ideas into action.

The conference room, adorned with symbols of Haiti's rich cultural heritage, hummed with the cadence of diverse languages. Delegates, dressed in suits adorned with colors echoing their cultural identities, engaged in discussions that transcended borders. Bishop Esperanza Ruiz, a figure of grace and wisdom, exchanged thoughts with Sheikh Ahmed Al-Farsi, representing the Islamic community with dignified poise. Rabbi Miriam Cohen, known for her ability to bridge gaps between faiths, contributed her insights to the unfolding dialogue.

Professor Sophie Moreau, a fervent educator passionate about change, animatedly shared visions of rebuilding Haiti's education system. Across the table, Marcus Turner, a seasoned investor with eyes that analyzed opportunities, contemplated the economic feasibility of potential projects. The room, a microcosm of diversity, echoed with the harmonious blend of expertise from various sectors – a symposium of minds united by a common goal.

President Laurent, her presence commanding attention, broke the anticipatory silence. "Ladies and gentlemen, we stand at the crossroads of history. Haiti calls out, and the world watches. Our task is not merely to rebuild but to reshape our destiny. Together, we can forge a path of prosperity, unity, and hope that will echo for future generations."

The moment's gravity settled over the gathering, and nods of agreement rippled through the room. The leaders, aware of the enormity of the task ahead, shared a collective understanding – the journey toward a peaceful solution for Haiti had commenced. Within the walls of this conference room, a mosaic of expertise, determination, and hope had assembled, poised to inscribe a new narrative for a nation poised for resurgence.

President Laurent, with a glance that embraced every soul present, continued, "Our collective wisdom is our greatest asset. Let us harness the power of collaboration, drawing strength from our diversity. We stand united, bound by the vision of a Haiti that rises, not just from the ruins of its challenges, but towards a future of boundless potential."

Now in full crescendo, the symphony of minds set the stage for what lay ahead. Ideas flowed like tributaries converging into a mighty river of purpose. The room was a crucible of change.

It became the birthplace of plans, dreams, and the firm commitment to weave a tapestry of strength, wealth, and unity for the people of Haiti. The journey had begun, and within the hearts and minds of these leaders, the first stitches of a new narrative were being carefully woven.

CHAPTER 10
THE HISTORY OF HAITI

As the leaders gathered in a quiet corner of their temporary headquarters, the conversation turned to the history of Haiti. Bishop Ruiz, with his gentle demeanor, began to speak, his voice carrying the weight of years past.

"Before we can understand where we are going, we must first understand where we come from," he said, his eyes reflecting the flickering candlelight. "Haiti's history is a complex tapestry of triumphs and tragedies, of resilience and resistance."

Annette leaned forward, her curiosity piqued. "Tell us more," she urged, her voice filled with anticipation.

Bishop Ruiz nodded, his thoughts drifting back to a time long ago. "Haiti was born out of revolution," he began, his voice steady. "In the late 18th century, enslaved Africans rose up against their oppressors, leading one of the most successful slave rebellions in history."

Marcus listened intently, his mind racing with questions. "And what followed?" he asked, his voice tinged with curiosity.

"After years of struggle and bloodshed, Haiti declared its independence in 1804, becoming the first black-led republic in the world," Bishop Ruiz continued, his words echoing with pride. "But the road to freedom was fraught with challenges. Haiti faced economic sanctions from European powers, crippling debt, and internal strife."

Professor Sophie nodded, her mind filled with images of resilience and determination. "Despite these challenges, Haiti continued to fight for its independence," she said, her voice filled with admiration.

Bishop Ruiz sighed, his thoughts turning to darker times. "But with independence came new struggles," he said, his voice tinged with sadness. "Political instability, corruption, and foreign intervention plagued the nation, leading to decades of unrest and violence."

Jean-Claude frowned, his mind grappling with the complexities of Haiti's history. "How did Haiti come to be in its current state?" he asked, his voice heavy with concern.

Bishop Ruiz paused, his thoughts drifting back to more recent events. "In the 20th century, Haiti experienced a series of dictators and military coups, further destabilizing the country," he explained, his voice filled with sorrow. "Corruption, poverty, and inequality became entrenched, creating a cycle of despair that has persisted to this day."

Sheikh Ahmed nodded solemnly, his heart heavy with the weight of Haiti's struggles. "But despite the challenges, Haiti's spirit remains unbroken," he said, his voice filled with conviction.

President Martine placed a hand on Sheikh Ahmed's shoulder, her eyes filled with determination. "That's why we're here," she said, her voice strong. "To help Haiti rise above its past and forge a new future."

As the leaders sat in silence, the echoes of Haiti's history lingered in the air. They knew that the road ahead would be difficult, but they were united in their determination to help Haiti break free from the chains of its past and embrace a brighter future.

CHAPTER 11
CONNECTING WITH THE HEART OF HAITI

As the leaders stepped out of the conference room, they were greeted by the bustling streets of Port-au-Prince. The sun beat down on the colorful buildings, and the air was filled with the sounds of laughter and conversation. It was clear that despite the challenges facing Haiti, there was a palpable sense of resilience and hope among its people.

Annette led the group through the streets, weaving through the bustling market stalls and lively neighborhoods. Along the way, they encountered members of the local community, each with their own stories and struggles.

Their first stop was a small school nestled in the heart of a bustling neighborhood. Children played in the courtyard, their laughter echoing off the walls. Annette introduced the leaders to the school's principal, who welcomed them with open arms.

"We've been working hard to improve the quality of education here," the principal explained, his voice filled with pride. "With the support of our community leaders and international partners, we've been able to provide better resources and opportunities for our students."

Professor Sophie engaged in a conversation with some of the teachers, discussing innovative teaching methods and strategies for supporting students from diverse backgrounds.

Meanwhile, Marcus spoke with the school's administrators about potential economic initiatives that could benefit the local community.

Next, the leaders visited a local community center, where they met with members of a women's cooperative. The women shared their experiences of running small businesses and the challenges they faced in accessing financial resources.

Jean-Claude listened intently, offering advice on how to access microfinance loans and navigate the complexities of the business world. "You have incredible potential," he said, his voice full of encouragement. "With the right support and resources, you can achieve great success."

Meanwhile, Sheikh Ahmed engaged in a dialogue with the women about the importance of economic empowerment and the role of women in society. "You are the backbone of your community," he said, his words resonating with warmth. "By supporting each other and working together, you can create a better future for yourselves and your families."

As the day went on, the leaders continued to interact with members of the local population, visiting community gardens, healthcare clinics, and cultural centers. Along the way, they listened to the stories of resilience and determination that defined Haiti's people.

Bishop Ruiz sat down with a group of community elders, listening to their stories of survival and perseverance in the face of adversity. "Your strength is an inspiration to us all," he said, his voice filled with reverence. "We are committed to working alongside you to build a brighter future for Haiti."

Rabbi Cohen joined a group of young musicians, sharing stories of his own cultural heritage and learning about the rich musical traditions of Haiti. "Music has the power to unite us all," he said, his eyes shining with admiration. "Together, we can create harmony out of chaos."

President Martine engaged in conversations with local leaders, discussing their vision for the future of Haiti and the role of collaboration in achieving it. "We are here to support you in your efforts," she said, her voice filled with determination. "Together, we can overcome any challenge that stands in our way."

As the sun began to set on the vibrant streets of Port-au-Prince, the leaders reflected on their interactions with the local population. They had witnessed firsthand the resilience, strength, and determination of Haiti's people, and they were more committed than ever to working alongside them to build a brighter future. As they walked back to their accommodations, they carried with them the stories and hopes of the local community, knowing that their journey was just beginning.

CHAPTER 12
SHADOWS WITHIN

In the dimly lit conference room, the leaders sat in a circle, their faces reflecting the weariness of their shared burden. Annette's brow furrowed with worry as she glanced around the room, her mind filled with doubts and uncertainties.

"Are we doing enough?" she wondered aloud, her voice barely above a whisper. "Can we truly make a difference in the face of such immense challenges?"

Marcus, usually the voice of reason, sighed heavily. "I find myself asking the same questions," he admitted, his gaze fixed on the floor. "Despite our best efforts, the economic situation remains dire, and the people continue to suffer."

Professor Sophie nodded in agreement, her usually bright eyes clouded with concern. "I fear that our education initiatives are falling short," she confessed, her voice tinged with sadness. "There are still so many children who lack access to quality education, and it weighs heavily on my conscience."

Jean-Claude, ever the pragmatist, shook his head in frustration. "Our economic strategies are sound on paper, but in practice, we face countless obstacles," he lamented, his voice tinged with frustration. "It's disheartening to see the same patterns of poverty and inequality persist despite our efforts."

Sheikh Ahmed, the embodiment of calm and wisdom, offered a reassuring smile. "Change takes time," he reminded them, his voice steady.

"We must remain patient and steadfast in our commitment to the cause. Rome was not built in a day, and neither will Haiti be transformed overnight."

Bishop Ruiz, the beacon of hope and compassion, placed a comforting hand on Annette's shoulder. "We must remember why we embarked on this journey in the first place," he said, his voice gentle. "To bring hope to the hopeless, to uplift the downtrodden, and to create a better future for all Haitians."

President Martine, the epitome of strength and resilience, nodded in agreement. "We knew from the beginning that this would not be easy," she said, her voice filled with determination. "But we cannot allow ourselves to be consumed by doubt or despair. We must press on, knowing that our efforts are not in vain."

As the leaders sat in silence, a sense of solidarity washed over them. They knew that their journey would be filled with challenges and setbacks, but they also knew that they were stronger together. With renewed determination, they rose from their seats, ready to face whatever obstacles lay ahead.

"We may be facing internal struggles," Annette said, her voice filled with conviction, "but we will not let them define us. We are united in our mission to bring about positive change, and together, we will overcome any obstacle in our path."

With those words ringing in their ears, the leaders left the conference room, their hearts filled with renewed hope and determination. They knew that the road ahead would not be easy, but they were ready to face whatever challenges came their way, knowing that they were not alone.

CHAPTER 13
RESOLVING INNER TURMOIL

As the coalition of leaders embarked on their mission to address the external challenges plaguing Haiti, they found themselves grappling with their own internal conflicts and tensions. Despite their shared vision and commitment to change, differing perspectives, personal agendas, and past grievances threatened to undermine their collective efforts.

Annette, fueled by her unwavering belief in the power of unity and community engagement, found herself at odds with Marcus, whose focus on economic empowerment sometimes overshadowed the importance of social cohesion and inclusivity. Their debates often sparked heated discussions within the group, as Annette advocated for a holistic approach that addressed both economic and social challenges, while Marcus remained steadfast in his belief that economic stability was the foundation for all other forms of progress.

Annette sighed, her frustration evident. "Marcus, I understand the importance of economic stability, but we can't ignore the social fabric of our communities. We need to prioritize inclusivity and address the needs of all Haitians, not just focus on economic metrics."

Marcus shook his head, his tone firm. "Annette, I hear what you're saying, but without a strong economy, we can't uplift our communities. We need to focus on creating jobs and fostering entrepreneurship to truly make a difference."

Meanwhile, Professor Sophie, driven by her passion for educational reform and youth empowerment, clashed with Jean-Claude, whose pragmatic approach to economic strategies sometimes overlooked the importance of investing in education and human capital. Their disagreements highlighted the tension between short-term economic goals and long-term social development, creating a rift within the group as they struggled to find common ground.

"I understand the need for economic growth, Jean-Claude, but education is the key to long-term prosperity," Professor Sophie argued, her voice tinged with frustration. "We can't neglect investing in our youth if we want to build a sustainable future for Haiti."

Jean-Claude nodded thoughtfully, but remained unconvinced. "Sophie, I agree that education is important, but we also need practical solutions to address immediate economic challenges. We can't afford to prioritize one over the other."

Sheikh Ahmed, known for his advocacy of interfaith collaboration and inclusivity, found himself at odds with Rabbi Cohen, whose focus on cultural preservation sometimes overshadowed the importance of embracing diversity and fostering unity among people of different faiths. Their debates often exposed deep-seated tensions rooted in historical grievances and cultural differences, threatening to fracture the coalition as they grappled with conflicting visions of a unified Haiti.

"We must celebrate our differences and work together as people of faith," Sheikh Ahmed urged, his voice calm but resolute. "Only through collaboration and understanding can we overcome the challenges facing our nation."

Rabbi Cohen nodded in agreement, but added, "Ahmed, while I agree with the importance of collaboration, we must also preserve our cultural heritage. It's what makes us unique and gives us strength."

Amidst these internal conflicts, Bishop Ruiz emerged as a voice of reason and reconciliation, urging the group to prioritize understanding and cooperation over division and discord. Drawing upon his experience in promoting social justice and healing, Bishop Ruiz facilitated open dialogue and mediation sessions, guiding the group towards a deeper appreciation of each other's perspectives and a shared commitment to overcoming their differences for the greater good of Haiti.

"It's natural to have differences of opinion, but we must remember our common goal: to uplift Haiti and its people," Bishop Ruiz said, his words resonating with wisdom. "Let us set aside our egos and work together for the greater good."

Through Bishop Ruiz's guidance and their collective determination to overcome internal strife, the leaders gradually navigated their way through conflicts, finding common ground and forging stronger bonds of trust and collaboration. As they confronted external challenges together, they realized that their unity in purpose and diversity of perspectives were their greatest strengths, laying the foundation for a more resilient and inclusive Haiti.

CHAPTER 14
SHADOWS OF DESPAIR

As the sun dipped below the Caribbean horizon, its final rays cast long shadows over the vibrant streets of Port-au-Prince. The air, heavy with a palpable sense of unease, carried with it the whispers of challenges that seemed to cling to Haiti like a stubborn shadow. Life pulsed through narrow alleys in the heart of the city. A community in that area found itself caught in the crosscurrents of big, unsolvable problems.

Children played barefoot within these labyrinthine streets. Their innocent laughter bounced off the crumbling walls that enclosed their makeshift homes. Yet, the purity of their joy stood in stark contrast to the harsh realities that lay just beyond their play area. People felt a tense atmosphere. Different factions vied for control. They turned the once-vibrant streets into a battleground for power.

Amidst this turmoil, a gathering unfolded in the dimly lit embrace of a community center. Sister Marie was a compassionate nun. She ran a modest school. She sat alongside Jean-Claude, a dedicated community organizer, and Annette, a resolute social worker. Their faces illuminated by a flickering candle, they huddled together, their minds determined to navigate the challenges that gripped their people like invisible chains.

Jean-Claude, his voice tinged with urgency, addressed the group, "The gangs are tightening their grip on our neighborhoods.

Our people are desperate, hungry, and have little access to education. We need to find a way to provide for them, to offer alternatives that break the cycle of violence."

Sister Marie, her eyes reflecting both sadness and unwavering resilience, added, "Our children should not grow up in fear. Education is the key, but we lack the necessary resources. We must find a way to open doors for them, to give them hope for a better future."

Annette, nodding in agreement, interjected with determination, "It's not just about dealing with the immediate threats; it's about addressing the root causes. The lack of opportunities and resources are driving our youth into the arms of these gangs. We need a holistic approach to break this vicious cycle."

As they shared their concerns and aspirations, a collective determination began to emerge within the group. Their vision transcended the current state of despair, painting a picture of a Haiti where the shadows of hopelessness would give way to the dawn of opportunity. In their minds, education and sustainable development weren't mere ideals; they were the antidotes to the stranglehold of violence that threatened to engulf their community.

In the midst of adversity, a flicker of hope ignited. The challenge ahead was immense, but the collective will of these local leaders burned brightly—a beacon pointing towards a future where the people of Haiti could reclaim their streets, their dignity, and their dreams. The dimly lit community center became a crucible of ideas, forging a path through the shadows of despair towards a horizon illuminated by the promise of a brighter tomorrow.

CHAPTER 15
CONVERGENCE OF MINDS

The tropical breeze stirred through the open windows of the community center, carrying with it the distant sounds of a city grappling with its challenges. Inside, the flickering candlelight cast a warm glow on the faces of Sister Marie, Jean-Claude, and Annette. The trio, driven by a shared determination, sat huddled around a worn wooden table, maps and blueprints spread before them.

Sister Marie's eyes, filled with compassion, surveyed the intricate details of the makeshift school she had lovingly nurtured over the years. "We must fortify our educational efforts," she emphasized, her voice a gentle yet persistent melody. "Education is the foundation upon which we build a future free from the shackles of ignorance and violence."

Jean-Claude, a beacon of community organizing, leaned forward. "I've been rallying support among local leaders. We need a united front against the gangs. It's time we establish community watch programs, emphasizing solidarity to counter the threats that loom in our streets."

With a fervor for social change, Annette contributed, "Beyond immediate security, we must address the economic disparity that fuels desperation. I've been in touch with local businesses and microfinance organizations. If we provide opportunities for entrepreneurship, we can empower our people to take control of their destinies."

They recognized the need for external support as their ideas melded into a cohesive plan. Sister Marie suggested, "Let us invite the international leaders who gathered with President Laurent. Their expertise could amplify our efforts, creating a convergence of minds that spans borders and cultures."

The trio worked tirelessly, drafting a letter of invitation to the global leaders. Their plea was not just for financial assistance but a partnership grounded in shared responsibility and empathy.

A team of educators and volunteers gathered in a nearby room, inspired by Sister Marie's vision. They envisioned transforming the small school into a beacon of knowledge, offering basic education and vocational training that could pave the way for meaningful employment.

As the night unfolded, a synergy of purpose enveloped the community center. The convergence of minds, fueled by the determination to uplift Haiti, spread beyond the local leaders to encompass a network of individuals committed to rewriting the narrative of their beloved nation.

Little did they know their journey had just begun. The challenges were immense, but the convergence of minds held the promise of a brighter future, where the resilience of the Haitian spirit would prevail over the shadows that loomed.

CHAPTER 16
THE CHALLENGE OF INTERNATIONAL COLLABORATION

In the lively neighborhoods and dynamic communities of Port-au-Prince, a diverse group of local and international leaders gathered in a sunlit conference room. President Martine Laurent sat at the head of the table, flanked by Annette, Marcus, Professor Sophie, Jean-Claude, Sheikh Ahmed, Bishop Ruiz, and Rabbi Cohen. Their mission was clear: to confront the pressing challenges facing Haiti and forge a path towards a brighter future. However, as they delved into discussions about collaboration, they quickly realized that navigating the complexities of working across cultural, political, and economic differences would be no easy task.

President Martine opened the meeting with a warm greeting, acknowledging the importance of collaboration in tackling Haiti's most pressing issues. "Thank you all for being here today," she began, her voice resonating with authority and determination. "As we embark on this journey together, it's crucial that we recognize the unique perspectives and expertise that each of us brings to the table. Only through open dialogue and mutual respect can we hope to overcome the challenges that lie ahead."

Annette, representing the local community, spoke next, emphasizing the importance of grassroots involvement in decision-making processes. "Our strength lies in our unity as a community," she said, her words infused with passion and conviction. "We must ensure that the voices of the people are heard and valued in our collaborative efforts. Only then can we truly create meaningful and sustainable change."

Marcus, known for his strategic thinking and economic insights, highlighted the need for a coordinated approach to addressing Haiti's economic challenges. "Economic empowerment is key to Haiti's prosperity," he asserted, his tone measured and confident. "By leveraging international resources and expertise, we can create opportunities for growth and development that benefit all members of society."

Professor Sophie, a champion for educational reform, stressed the importance of investing in Haiti's youth. "Education is the cornerstone of progress," she stated, her voice unwavering. "We must work together to ensure that every child has access to quality education, regardless of their background or circumstances. Only then can we unlock Haiti's full potential."

Jean-Claude, drawing upon his experience as an economist, spoke about the need for inclusive economic policies that promote sustainable development. "We must be mindful of the impact our decisions have on the most vulnerable members of society," he urged, his tone pragmatic yet empathetic. "By prioritizing inclusive growth, we can build a more resilient and equitable Haiti."

Sheikh Ahmed, representing the Islamic community, emphasized the importance of interfaith collaboration in fostering unity and understanding. "In times of crisis, it's crucial that we come together as people of faith," he said, his voice calm and reassuring. "By embracing our shared humanity and working towards common goals, we can overcome any obstacle that stands in our way."

Bishop Ruiz, a figure of wisdom and compassion, echoed Sheikh Ahmed's sentiments, emphasizing the power of unity in times of adversity. "Our diversity is our strength," he declared, his words imbued with a sense of hope and optimism. "Together, we can overcome the challenges that lie ahead and build a brighter future for Haiti."

Rabbi Cohen, known for his advocacy of cultural preservation, spoke about the importance of honoring Haiti's rich cultural heritage. "Our cultural identity is what makes us unique," he asserted, his voice filled with pride. "By celebrating our diversity and embracing our differences, we can create a more inclusive and harmonious society."

As the leaders engaged in dialogue, exchanging ideas and perspectives, they encountered challenges along the way. Cultural differences, language barriers, and divergent political ideologies threatened to derail their collaborative efforts at times. However, through patience, understanding, and a shared commitment to their mission, they were able to overcome these obstacles and forge stronger bonds of trust and cooperation.

As the diverse group of leaders concluded their meeting in Port-au-Prince, the positive outcomes of their collaborative efforts quickly garnered attention from international bodies eager to support Haiti's progress.

In a virtual conference room halfway across the globe, representatives from various international organizations tuned in to hear about the promising developments in Haiti. Among them was Maria Rodriguez, the Director of International Development at the United Nations Development Programme (UNDP).

Impressed by the proactive approach taken by the local and international leaders, Maria expressed her organization's readiness to assist Haiti in its journey towards a brighter future. "It's inspiring to see such dedication and determination among the leaders in Haiti," she remarked, her voice projecting through the conference call. "The UNDP stands ready to provide support in areas such as infrastructure development, capacity-building, and sustainable economic growth. Together, we can make a tangible difference in the lives of the Haitian people."

Her sentiments were echoed by John Smith, a representative from the World Bank, who emphasized the importance of coordinated efforts in addressing Haiti's complex challenges. "Collaboration is key to unlocking Haiti's potential," he affirmed, nodding in agreement with Maria's remarks. "The World Bank is committed to working closely with our partners in Haiti to implement projects that promote inclusive growth and poverty reduction. By pooling our resources and expertise, we can achieve meaningful impact."

Back in Port-au-Prince, President Martine Laurent and her fellow leaders listened intently to the words of support from their international counterparts. Encouraged by the positive response, they reaffirmed their commitment to working together towards a common vision of prosperity and stability for Haiti.

"I am grateful for the support and solidarity shown by our international partners," President Martine declared, her voice filled with gratitude. "Together, we can overcome the challenges that lie ahead and build a brighter future for Haiti. Let us continue to work hand in hand, united in our determination to create positive change."

The room buzzed with a sense of optimism as the leaders exchanged smiles and words of encouragement. The collaborative spirit that had guided their meeting in Port-au-Prince now extended to the international stage, signaling a new chapter of cooperation and progress for Haiti.

In the end, the leaders emerged from the meeting with a renewed sense of purpose and determination. They had laid the groundwork for a collaborative partnership that would transcend borders and boundaries, uniting local and international leaders in their shared quest to build a brighter future for Haiti. As they stepped out into the sunlit streets of Port-au-Prince, they knew that their journey was just beginning, but they faced the challenges ahead with hope, resilience, and a steadfast commitment to collaboration.

CHAPTER 17
FORGING UNITY

The sunlight made Port-au-Prince look warm and hopeful, even though the area had faced many challenges. A new plan was forming in the middle of the city, where busy streets met calm alleys. People were coming together to create this plan because they believed that working together could solve the problems in their community.

President Martine Laurent stood on the steps of the National Palace, addressing a diverse crowd that had gathered in front of the iconic structure. Her voice, a blend of conviction and compassion, echoed through the air. "My fellow Haitians, today marks a turning point in our history. We stand united against the forces that seek to divide us. It's time to forge a path of solidarity and resilience."

The crowd, comprised of diverse faces representing the vibrant diversity of Haitian culture, listened attentively. Among them were educators, religious leaders, community organizers, and everyday citizens – each carrying a story of perseverance.

Jean-Claude Desmarais, the renowned economist, stepped forward. "Unity must extend beyond our words; it must be woven into the fabric of our society. We have devised a comprehensive economic plan that fosters inclusivity and empowers local businesses. Together, we can build an economy that lifts everyone."

The meticulously crafted plan emphasized sustainable development and equitable distribution of resources. It aimed to create opportunities transcending class and background, fostering an environment where prosperity was not a distant dream but a tangible reality.

Standing alongside leaders from various faiths, Bishop Esperanza Ruiz raised her voice in a prayer for unity. "In the eyes of the divine, we are all children of the same universe. Let our differences be a source of strength, not division. Together, we can overcome any challenge that befalls us."

Inspired by the words of hope and guided by the spirit of unity, the crowd began to disperse, each carrying a renewed sense of purpose. Once fragmented by internal strife, the city witnessed the seeds of a collective effort taking root. In the following days, workshops and town hall meetings became the nexus of dialogue. Local leaders, representatives from different sectors, and concerned citizens engaged in discussions beyond the superficial. They delved into the root causes of societal issues, seeking holistic solutions that addressed their community's intricate web of challenges.

Jean-Claude, the community organizer, spearheaded efforts to establish neighborhood committees. These grassroots initiatives became the eyes and ears of the community, fostering a sense of camaraderie that stood as a bulwark against the encroaching influence of gangs.

Sister Marie's school was transformed into a haven of knowledge and inspiration. With the support of international leaders, the modest institution blossomed into a center of excellence, offering not only academic education but also vocational training. Students, once confined by the limitations of circumstance, now glimpse a future filled with possibilities.

Annette's vision of economic empowerment began to take shape. Local businesses received support and guidance, while microfinance initiatives provided a lifeline to budding entrepreneurs. Once paralyzed by fear, the bustling marketplace now buzzed with activity as commerce and hope intertwined.

The seasoned investor, Marcus Turner facilitated connections between international corporations and local enterprises. His strategic alliances brought much-needed resources, injecting vitality into the veins of the Haitian economy.

The cityscape transformed physically and in the hearts and minds of its inhabitants. Murals depicting unity and resilience adorned the walls, serving as a constant reminder of the collective journey embarked upon by the people.

As the months passed, the fruits of their labor became evident. Crime rates dwindled, education flourished, and the economy experienced a renaissance. Haiti, once a symbol of struggle, emerged as a testament to the power of unity.

President Martine Laurent stood once again before the National Palace, surveying the transformed city with a sense of pride. "We have proven that when we stand together, there is no challenge too great, no obstacle insurmountable. Let this be a beacon of hope for the world – the story of a nation that refused to be defined by its hardships but instead forged unity as the cornerstone of its future."

And so, the journey continued, with the people of Haiti walking hand in hand towards a destiny of their own making – a destiny forged in unity, resilience, and the unwavering belief that their collective strength could overcome any adversity.

CHAPTER 18
WHISPERS IN THE SHADOWS

As the sun dipped below the horizon, Port-au-Prince revealed a different side to itself – a city cloaked in shadows, where the struggles of the day seemed to fester and multiply. In the narrow alleys and dimly lit corners, whispers of discontent and fear echoed through the night, giving voice to the challenges that lingered in the shadows.

Sister Marie, clad in her nun's habit, walked through the labyrinthine streets, her heart heavy with the weight of the secrets concealed in the darkness. She had heard whispers of a new gang rising, a formidable force threatening to undo the progress that unity had begun to build. The very shadows they sought to dispel were now teeming with unseen adversaries.

The once-vibrant neighborhood, which had embraced hope like a long-lost friend, now bore the scars of a resurgence in criminal activities. Graffiti adorned walls, marking territories where fear held sway. The air buzzed with tension, and the laughter of children playing in the daytime had given way to an eerie silence.

Sister Marie, Jean-Claude, and Annette gathered in the dimly lit community center, their faces reflecting a mix of determination and concern. The unity they had forged seemed to be slipping through their fingers, and the shadows whispered of a looming threat that required immediate attention.

Jean-Claude, his brow furrowed, spoke first, "We cannot let this darkness swallow the progress we've made. We need to understand the root of this resurgence, expose it, and root it out."

Annette nodded in agreement, "The economic empowerment we've been working towards – it's the key. Desperation breeds these gangs. If we can offer viable alternatives, we can undermine their appeal."

Sister Marie, her eyes reflecting both sorrow and resolve, added, "But we must also address the emotional wounds of our community. The scars run deep, and healing requires more than economic measures. We need to offer hope, restore a sense of security, and let our people know they are not alone."

Their plan took shape in the form of a multifaceted approach. Jean-Claude mobilized community patrols, ordinary citizens who, armed with determination and a commitment to their neighborhoods, became the eyes and ears against the encroaching darkness. Annette intensified her efforts to connect local businesses with international partners, creating a network that could provide jobs and economic stability.

Sister Marie, with a heart dedicated to healing, initiated support groups and counseling services. The echoes of trauma, hidden in the shadows, began to surface as individuals shared their stories and found solace in a community that refused to be defined by fear.

In the midst of this struggle, a surprising ally emerged. Marcus Turner, the seasoned investor, recognized that the economic resurgence they sought was not immune to the shadows. He used his influence to engage corporations in a pact of social responsibility, urging them to invest not just in profit but in the well-being of the communities they operated in.

The alliance between the community leaders and the corporate world brought resources and expertise to the forefront. A once-unseen force, operating in the shadows, began to feel the pressure of a united front.

As days turned into weeks, the whispers of discontent diminished. The patrols proved effective, reclaiming streets that had been surrendered to fear. Economic opportunities flourished, giving the youth a path away from the allure of the gangs. Sister Marie's healing initiatives, supported by the newfound corporate partnerships, began to mend the emotional wounds that had festered in the shadows.

The community center, once a hub of despair, became a symbol of resilience. Walls adorned not only with murals of hope but with the faces of those who refused to be silenced by the whispers in the shadows.

Sister Marie, Jean-Claude, and Annette stood together, surveying the revitalized neighborhood. The scars of the recent threat were fading, replaced by a palpable sense of triumph. The shadows still existed, but they were no longer insurmountable – they were now spaces waiting to be filled with the light of progress.

In the quiet of the night, as the city slept, the echoes of their collective effort lingered. The whispers in the shadows had been drowned out by the resounding chorus of a community that had found its voice, refusing to be defined by the darkness that sought to consume it.

CHAPTER 19
THREADS OF HOPE

The morning sun painted the sky in hues of gold, signaling the beginning of a new day in Port-au-Prince. In the heart of the city, Sister Marie, Jean-Claude, and Annette gathered once again in the community center, their faces reflecting a mixture of weariness and determination. Today, their focus shifted towards a different battle – the battle against despair that had woven its threads into the fabric of their community.

Around a worn wooden table, strewn with maps and plans, they convened to address the emotional wounds that lingered. The recent resurgence of criminal activities had left scars not only on the streets but on the hearts of the people they were striving to uplift.

Jean-Claude spoke, his voice steady, "The patrols are making progress, and the economic initiatives are taking root, but we can't ignore the pain that runs deep. We need to offer more than just security and jobs; we need to weave threads of hope into the very essence of our community."

Sister Marie, her eyes filled with compassion, nodded in agreement, "Despair has a way of unraveling the spirit. We must find ways to mend the fabric of our community, to offer support that goes beyond the physical."

Annette, ever pragmatic, added, "We can leverage the partnerships we've formed. The corporations have resources, and the international leaders might have insights on initiatives that have worked elsewhere. Let's explore avenues for comprehensive support."

Their plan took shape – a holistic approach that aimed not only to heal wounds but to fortify the resilience of the community. The worn-out chairs creaked as they leaned in, delving into the specifics of their new endeavor.

Days turned into weeks, and the community center transformed into a hub of hope. Support groups, led by Sister Marie, became a safe space for individuals to share their experiences, fears, and dreams. The community, once fragmented by the shadows, now found solace in collective understanding.

Jean-Claude, with the support of local artists, initiated a mural project. Vibrant colors adorned the walls, depicting the stories of triumph over adversity. Each stroke of paint became a thread, weaving tales of resilience that whispered promises of a brighter future.

Annette, with a keen eye for sustainable initiatives, established vocational training programs. The hum of sewing machines echoed through the community center as individuals learned the art of craftsmanship. The products created not only provided economic opportunities but served as symbols of the community's creativity and determination.

After a while, the impact of their efforts became evident. The once-muted laughter of children returned to the streets. The murals, like sentinels, stood guard against the encroaching shadows.

The vocational training graduates, now skilled artisans, showcased their creations at a local market, their faces radiating pride.

One evening, under the soft glow of the community center's lights, an impromptu gathering took place. The room buzzed with energy as locals shared their stories of personal triumphs. Sister Marie, beaming with joy, witnessed the transformation of pain into resilience.

Amidst the celebration, a familiar face appeared at the doorway. President Martine Laurent stood; her eyes filled with admiration. "I've heard of the incredible work happening here," she said, joining the gathering. "The threads of hope you've woven are turning into a tapestry of inspiration for the entire nation."

The community leaders, once again united, expressed their gratitude for the support of international leaders and local businesses. President Laurent, recognizing the significance of their collective endeavor, pledged continued assistance in ensuring that the threads of hope would endure, strengthening the fabric of the community for generations to come.

As the night unfolded, laughter mingled with the music of the streets, creating a symphony of resilience. The community center, once a battleground against despair, now stood as a testament to the transformative power of hope.

In the quiet hours of the night, as the city settled into a peaceful slumber, the threads of hope continued to weave their way through Port-au-Prince. The battle against despair was ongoing, but the community had discovered a potent weapon – a collective spirit that could mend even the most frayed threads and create a tapestry of resilience that would endure through time.

CHAPTER 20
ECONOMIC RESURGENCE

The morning sun painted the sky with hues of amber as Port-au-Prince stirred with a renewed sense of purpose. In the heart of the city, a gathering took place at the community center, where the leaders – President Martine Laurent, Jean-Claude Desmarais, Marcus Turner, and Annette – convened to propel their economic initiatives to greater heights.

Jean-Claude Desmarais, the seasoned economist, stood at the front of the room, the table strewn with blueprints and financial reports serving as his podium. As he prepared to address the gathering at the community center, he felt a surge of determination coursing through him. The economic resurgence of Port-au-Prince was not just a concept; it was a mission he was deeply committed to.

"Good morning, everyone," Jean-Claude began, his voice carrying the weight of experience and conviction. "Thank you for joining us today to discuss our ongoing economic initiatives and how we can further propel our community towards prosperity."

A murmur of agreement rippled through the audience, a diverse group of community members, entrepreneurs, and local leaders gathered to hear about the progress and future plans for economic growth.

Jean-Claude continued, "Our economic plan has shown promise, but we recognize that there are challenges we must address to ensure that the benefits of our initiatives reach every corner of our community.

I'm here today to hear your feedback, answer your questions, and work together to find solutions."

A hand shot up from the crowd, and Jean-Claude nodded in acknowledgment.

"Mr. Desmarais, how do you plan to ensure that small businesses, especially those in underserved areas, have access to the resources and support they need to thrive?" a woman in the audience asked, her voice tinged with concern.

Jean-Claude paused for a moment, considering the question carefully. "Thank you for that important question. One of our primary objectives is to create a supportive ecosystem for small businesses, particularly in neighborhoods that have historically lacked access to economic opportunities."

He went on to outline specific initiatives aimed at providing financial assistance, mentorship programs, and access to markets for local entrepreneurs. As he spoke, he could see nods of approval and thoughtful expressions among the audience members, reassured by his commitment to their economic empowerment.

Another question came from a young man seated in the front row. "Mr. Desmarais, how do you intend to address the issue of unemployment, especially among the youth population?"

Jean-Claude nodded, acknowledging the significance of the question. "Unemployment, particularly among our youth, is a pressing concern that requires a multi-faceted approach. In addition to creating job opportunities through our economic initiatives, we're also focused on investing in vocational training programs and educational initiatives to equip our young people with the skills they need for meaningful employment."

He went on to explain the specifics of the vocational training programs and partnerships with educational institutions that were already underway, emphasizing the importance of preparing the next generation for success in a rapidly evolving economy.

As the discussion continued, Jean-Claude fielded questions on topics ranging from infrastructure development to environmental sustainability, demonstrating his depth of knowledge and his unwavering commitment to addressing the needs of the community.

By the end of the session, Jean-Claude felt a sense of satisfaction knowing that the economic resurgence of Port-au-Prince was not just a vision he articulated but a collective effort driven by the needs and aspirations of the people he served.

Marcus Turner, his demeanor a blend of confidence and calculation, nodded in agreement. "I've been in talks with several corporations interested in investing in community-driven projects. Our challenge is to align their goals with the needs and aspirations of our people."

President Laurent, a beacon of leadership, interjected, "Our people need more than just jobs; they need opportunities to thrive. Education and training programs should run parallel to our economic initiatives, ensuring that the benefits are not temporary but enduring."

Their discussion delved into the specifics of projects that would stimulate economic resurgence. Jean-Claude emphasized the importance of developing sectors that aligned with the skills and resources of the community. Annette proposed creating a local business hub where entrepreneurs could access support and mentorship.

Marcus shared insights from his conversations with international investors, outlining potential collaborations that could inject capital into the local economy. President Laurent, nodding approvingly, suggested incorporating sustainable practices into the economic plan to ensure long-term benefits for both the community and the environment.

The room buzzed with ideas and ambition as the leaders mapped out a comprehensive strategy. The economic resurgence they envisioned wasn't merely about numbers; it was about transforming the lives of the people who called Port-au-Prince home.

Annette, with her pragmatic approach, added, "We've established connections with local businesses, but it's time to expand our reach. Marcus, your expertise in forging international partnerships will be crucial in securing resources and opportunities."

After the meeting concluded, Jean-Claude lingered for a moment, exchanging words of encouragement and gratitude with the attendees. As he stepped out into the sunlight streaming through the windows of the community center, he knew that the path to economic prosperity was paved with challenges, but with the support of the community, he was confident they would overcome them together.

In the weeks that followed, the economic initiatives unfolded like a symphony of progress. The local business hub, a bustling space filled with entrepreneurs and innovators, became a nucleus of creativity and collaboration. Annette, with her team, provided guidance and resources, nurturing the growth of small enterprises that echoed with the spirit of the community.

Jean-Claude, in partnership with local educational institutions, initiated vocational training programs. The programs were tailored to meet the demands of emerging industries, ensuring that the workforce was equipped with the skills needed for sustainable employment.

Marcus, leveraging his international connections, attracted investments that catalyzed the development of infrastructure projects. Factories, schools, and sustainable housing began to rise, transforming the cityscape and providing a tangible representation of the economic resurgence.

One day, President Laurent stood before a newly inaugurated manufacturing facility, its sleek architecture a testament to the fusion of modernity and community. The facility, powered by clean energy, employed locals, and produced goods for both local and international markets.

"This is not just a factory," President Laurent declared, addressing the crowd gathered for the inauguration. "This is a symbol of what we can achieve when we harness our collective potential. Our economic resurgence is not measured solely in profits but in the opportunities, it creates for our people."

The impact of the economic initiatives rippled through the community. The once-neglected neighborhoods saw a transformation – new businesses, renovated schools, and affordable housing developments. The vibrancy of economic activity breathed life into the city, dispelling the shadows of unemployment and poverty.

Yet, amidst the progress, the leaders were cognizant of the need to ensure inclusivity. They held town hall meetings, engaging with the community to gather feedback and address concerns.

President Laurent emphasized the importance of transparency and accountability in the implementation of their economic plan.

As the economic resurgence gained momentum, the leaders faced new challenges. Maintaining a delicate balance between progress and preserving the cultural identity of the community became a priority. Annette, always attuned to the pulse of the people, championed initiatives that celebrated local art, traditions, and craftsmanship.

The community center, once a hub for discussions, evolved into a business incubator, supporting aspiring entrepreneurs with mentorship programs and access to funding. The vision of economic resurgence, conceived around a table strewn with blueprints, became a reality that touched the lives of every citizen.

The leaders, as they observed the transformative impact of their initiatives, knew that the journey was ongoing. The economic resurgence wasn't a destination but a continuous effort to uplift the community and lay the foundation for a sustainable and prosperous future.

As the sun set over Port-au-Prince, casting a warm glow over the city, the leaders stood together, surveying the changes they had catalyzed. The economic resurgence was not just about bricks and mortar; it was about empowering individuals, fostering dreams, and igniting a beacon of hope that would continue to shine brightly in the hearts of the people.

CHAPTER 21
STREETS OF DETERMINATION

The recent economic resurgence, while bringing tangible improvements, also unearthed challenges embedded in the very fabric of the community. Sister Marie, Jean-Claude, Annette, and a group of local leaders convened at the community center to address the pressing issue – the determination of the streets.

The room echoed with the sounds of passionate discussion as they grappled with the complexities of the challenges that lingered in the shadows of progress. Jean-Claude, his voice resonant with determination, spoke first, "Our economic initiatives are transforming the city, but the streets are a reflection of the struggles we cannot ignore. The battle for our community's soul is being fought in these alleys, and we need a strategy to reclaim them."

Sister Marie, her eyes reflecting both compassion and concern, added, "The transformation should not bypass those who walk the streets every day. We need to address the root causes of the challenges – poverty, homelessness, addiction – with empathy and a commitment to uplift."

Annette, pragmatic as always, interjected, "We've created jobs and economic opportunities, but for some, the journey is still uphill. Let's focus on creating social programs that provide support for those facing the toughest battles."

The conversation delved into the nuances of the challenges. The leaders recognized that the streets were not just physical spaces, but embodiments of the struggles faced by individuals – battles against poverty, addiction, and a lack of access to resources.

As they brainstormed solutions, a consensus emerged on the need for holistic programs that tackled the multifaceted nature of the issues. Jean-Claude proposed community outreach programs that would connect with the most vulnerable, offering a helping hand and a pathway to recovery. Annette suggested partnerships with rehabilitation centers and mental health organizations to address the deeper layers of the challenges.

The leaders, fueled by their collective determination, decided to take to the streets themselves. They organized a series of town hall meetings, inviting the community to share their stories, struggles, and aspirations. The gatherings became a platform for dialogue, a space where the voices of the streets could be heard.

In one such meeting, held in the heart of a neighborhood that bore the weight of poverty, Sister Marie listened as individuals poured their hearts out. A young woman, her eyes reflecting both resilience and pain, spoke about the challenges of raising a family with limited resources. A man, who had battled addiction and emerged victorious, shared his journey towards recovery.

Moved by these stories, Sister Marie envisioned a haven for those seeking refuge from the harsh realities of the streets. She proposed the creation of a community center specifically designed to provide support for vulnerable populations – a place where individuals facing homelessness, addiction, or mental health struggles could find resources, counseling, and a sense of belonging.

Annette, leveraging her connections in the business community, secured funding for the project. The community center, with its doors wide open, became a beacon of hope in the heart of the city. It offered not only practical support but also a network of individuals determined to break the cycles of adversity.

Jean-Claude, in collaboration with local law enforcement, initiated community policing programs. Officers, familiar faces in the neighborhoods, worked alongside residents to ensure that the streets were safe and that those in need related to the resources available.

The community center, aptly named "Streets of Determination," became a symbol of the resilience of the people it served. It offered job training programs, mental health counseling, and a platform for artistic expression. Sister Marie, now overseeing the center, welcomed everyone with open arms, fostering a sense of community and collective determination.

As the months passed, the impact of the Streets of Determination initiative resonated through the alleys and lanes of Port-au-Prince. The individuals who once walked the streets with weariness now found solace and support. The sense of determination that had fueled the leaders in their discussions permeated the very essence of the community.

One evening, President Martine Laurent visited the Streets of Determination community center. She walked through its halls, witnessing the transformation that had taken place. Individuals who had once been defined by their struggles now stood as beacons of determination and resilience.

Addressing the gathered crowd, President Laurent spoke, "The streets are no longer just a battleground for survival; they are pathways of hope and opportunity.

The determination we see here today is a testament to the strength of our community."

The leaders, standing side by side, recognized that the journey was far from over. The streets, once symbols of struggle, now bore witness to the indomitable spirit of a community united in its determination to uplift every member, regardless of the challenges they faced.

As they stepped back into the city, the streets echoed with a new narrative – one of collective determination, empathy, and the unwavering belief that every individual, regardless of their past, could find a path toward a brighter future.

CHAPTER 22
SISTER MARIE'S SCHOOL OF DREAMS

A modest building stood with a weathered sign that read, "Sister Marie's School of Dreams." The school, born from the vision of Sister Marie and supported by the community leaders, represented a beacon of hope and education for the children of the city.

Inside the school, the air was filled with the hum of learning and the laughter of children eager to explore the realms of knowledge. Sister Marie, wearing her habit with grace, moved through the classrooms, observing the vibrant energy that filled the spaces. She believed that education was not just about imparting knowledge; it was a tool to nurture dreams and transform lives.

One morning, in the small courtyard where students gathered for assembly, Sister Marie addressed the eager faces before her. "My dear students, welcome to another day of exploration and discovery. In this school, each of you is not just a student; you are a dreamer, and this is your School of Dreams."

The children, from diverse backgrounds, listened with wide-eyed enthusiasm. Sister Marie continued, "In your hearts, you carry dreams – dreams of becoming doctors, artists, engineers, and leaders who will shape the future of our community. Here, we nurture those dreams, providing the knowledge and support needed to turn them into reality."

The School of Dreams was not just a place of academic learning; it was a hub of creativity and inspiration. The curriculum extended beyond textbooks, incorporating arts, music, and activities that encouraged the children to explore their passions.

As the school year progressed, Sister Marie's vision extended beyond the classroom walls. She collaborated with local artists to create murals that adorned the school, depicting scenes of hope, unity, and the dreams that each child aspired to achieve. The murals became a testament to the power of education in shaping a brighter future.

Jean-Claude, recognizing the importance of holistic development, initiated mentorship programs that paired students with professionals from various fields. The children had the opportunity to engage with role models who shared their experiences and encouraged them to dream big.

One day, Annette visited the School of Dreams, accompanied by Marcus Turner. They toured the classrooms, witnessed the vibrant activities, and engaged with the students. Annette, with a smile, spoke to a group of young aspiring entrepreneurs, "Your dreams are not just aspirations; they are the seeds of a future where you can achieve anything you set your minds to. The community believes in you, and we are here to support your journey."

Marcus, inspired by the enthusiasm of the students, shared stories of his own journey in the business world. He spoke about the importance of perseverance, resilience, and the belief that dreams could be transformed into tangible achievements with dedication and hard work.

The School of Dreams also became a focal point for community engagement. Regular events, such as cultural festivals and open houses, welcomed parents, guardians, and community members to witness the growth and potential of the students. The school, once a hidden gem, became a source of pride for the entire community.

As the school year culminated, Sister Marie organized a grand celebration – a culmination of dreams, achievements, and the spirit of community. The courtyard, adorned with colorful decorations, buzzed with excitement as students prepared to showcase their talents.

Bishop Esperanza Ruiz, Sheikh Ahmed Al-Farsi, and Rabbi Miriam Cohen, recognizing the significance of education in fostering understanding, attended the celebration. They spoke about the unity that education could bring, transcending religious and cultural boundaries. Together, they symbolically cut a ribbon, inaugurating a new wing of the School of Dreams dedicated to cultural exchange and understanding.

The students, dressed in a kaleidoscope of colors, took the stage. They recited poems, performed traditional dances, and showcased their artwork. The audience, consisting of parents, community members, and the leaders who had supported the school, erupted in applause.

President Martine Laurent, who had championed education as a cornerstone of progress, addressed the gathering, "The School of Dreams is not just a place of learning; it is a testament to the potential that resides within each child. Education is the key that unlocks doors, and as a community, we are committed to providing that key to every child, regardless of their background."

Sister Marie, standing amidst the jubilant celebration, reflected on the journey of the School of Dreams. It had become more than an educational institution; it was a symbol of collective determination, unity, and the belief that every child had the right to dream and pursue those dreams.

As the celebration continued, the sun dipped below the horizon, casting a warm glow over the School of Dreams. The children, with hearts full of aspirations, continued to dream, and the leaders, standing together, recognized that the investment in education was an investment in a future where the dreams of the community could flourish and illuminate the path to progress.

CHAPTER 23
JEAN-CLAUDE'S BLUEPRINT

Jean-Claude Desmarais, the visionary economist, called upon the community leaders for a meeting at the community center. The air buzzed with anticipation as Jean-Claude unfurled a blueprint that represented not just economic development but a transformative vision for the future of the city.

The leaders, seated around the table strewn with charts and graphs, fixed their gaze on Jean-Claude. "My friends," he began, his voice carrying a mix of determination and excitement, "we've made incredible strides in revitalizing the economy, but now it's time to set our sights on a grander vision. This blueprint outlines a comprehensive plan that goes beyond incremental progress; it's about shaping the destiny of Port-au-Prince."

Annette, with her pragmatic approach, leaned forward. "What are the key components of this blueprint, Jean-Claude? We need a roadmap that not only brings prosperity but ensures inclusivity and sustainability."

Jean-Claude nodded, his eyes gleaming with enthusiasm. "The blueprint encompasses three pillars: Sustainable Urban Development, Technological Innovation, and Social Equity. Each pillar supports the others, creating a foundation for a city that thrives in every aspect."

The leaders, eager to delve into the details, engaged in a dialogue that would shape the trajectory of Port-au-Prince.

Jean-Claude emphasized the need to reimagine the cityscape. "We will focus on creating green spaces, promoting eco-friendly architecture, and revitalizing neglected neighborhoods. Our goal is not just a visually appealing city but one that fosters a sense of pride and well-being among its residents."

Annette, considering the economic implications, suggested, "Let's ensure that our sustainable initiatives also create job opportunities. Green projects, such as urban gardens and renewable energy initiatives, cannot only enhance the city but also contribute to the economic empowerment of our community."

Marcus Turner, always attuned to the possibilities of progress, spoke, "Technological innovation will be the engine driving our city forward. We can invest in smart infrastructure, digital connectivity, and initiatives that position Port-au-Prince as a hub for technological advancements."

Jean-Claude added, "Education will play a crucial role. We must invest in STEM programs, coding workshops, and initiatives that prepare our youth for the jobs of the future. The School of Dreams can be a cornerstone in nurturing the next generation of innovators."

Sister Marie, the voice of compassion, emphasized the importance of social equity. "Our blueprint must ensure that the benefits of progress are accessible to all. Initiatives that address poverty, healthcare, and social inclusion should be integrated into the very fabric of our plan."

Bishop Esperanza Ruiz, Sheikh Ahmed Al-Farsi, and Rabbi Miriam Cohen, representing different faiths, expressed their support for initiatives that promoted unity and understanding among diverse communities.

The blueprint, as it unfolded, became a roadmap for a city that balanced progress with humanity.

After about six months, the blueprint evolved into a tangible plan. The community leaders, in collaboration with urban planners, architects, and technologists, worked tirelessly to breathe life into Jean-Claude's vision.

Green spaces emerged, transforming neglected areas into vibrant community hubs. Rooftop gardens adorned buildings, providing not just aesthetic value but also sustainable food sources. The once-ignored neighborhoods became focal points for cultural expression, with local artists contributing to the revitalization.

Technological innovation became evident in the smart infrastructure that dotted the city. Public spaces were equipped with Wi-Fi, and initiatives like a city-wide app simplified access to services. The School of Dreams, now a tech-savvy institution, became a model for integrating technology into education.

Social equity initiatives addressed longstanding challenges. Healthcare clinics, supported by local and international partnerships, provide accessible and affordable healthcare. Job training programs, in collaboration with businesses, created pathways for employment, ensuring that the economic benefits of progress reached every corner of the community.

Annette, leveraging her connections, secured funding for the initiatives, engaging not only local businesses but also international organizations committed to sustainable development. The blueprint, once a vision on paper, became a collaborative effort that transcended borders.

As the transformation unfolded, President Martine Laurent visited Port-au-Prince to witness the changes. She stood amidst the green spaces, observed the technological advancements, and engaged with community members benefiting from the social equity initiatives. "This is not just progress; it's a testament to what a community can achieve when they dream collectively and work towards a shared vision."

The leaders, as they surveyed the city, they had helped shape, recognized that Jean-Claude's blueprint had not only revitalized Port-au-Prince but had set a precedent for urban development worldwide.

One evening, a grand unveiling ceremony took place in the heart of the city. The leaders, alongside community members, watched as the blueprint became a symbol of the city's resilience and determination. The once-bustling streets now reflected a city that had not just been rebuilt but had redefined its identity.

Jean-Claude, addressing the gathered crowd, spoke with pride, "Port-au-Prince is not just a city; it's a testament to the power of collective vision. We've created a blueprint for progress that goes beyond infrastructure – it's about nurturing the soul of our community."

As the sun set over the transformed city, casting a warm glow on the green spaces and technological marvels, the leaders stood together. The blueprint, now a living reality, symbolized the endless possibilities that unfold when a community dares to dream and takes collective steps towards a brighter future.

CHAPTER 24
INVESTING IN TOMORROW

In the opulent boardroom perched high above the transformed cityscape of Port-au-Prince, Marcus Turner, a beacon of determination and foresight, stood before a gathering of investors. The room, adorned with panoramic windows revealing the urban metamorphosis below, set the stage for a pivotal moment in the narrative of progress.

"Port-au-Prince is no longer just a city; it's a testament to what strategic investments can achieve," Marcus declared, his voice carrying the weight of conviction. The investors, seated around the sleek table, absorbed the significance of his words. "Our initiatives in sustainable development, technological innovation, and social equity have not only revitalized the community but created a blueprint for a brighter future."

The city below, once marred by shadows, now pulsated with life and promise. A transformation, born out of a collective vision and commitment to change, unfolded like a tapestry beneath the gaze of the boardroom.

Marcus continued, "Investing in tomorrow means not only securing financial returns but building a legacy of progress, unity, and resilience for generations to come. Our responsibility extends beyond the balance sheets; it encompasses the lives touched, the communities uplifted, and the sustainable practices that safeguard our shared future."

Around the table, heads nodded in acknowledgment. The investors, drawn to Marcus's unwavering belief in the transformative power of strategic investments, were eager to hear the narrative of success that had unfolded under his stewardship.

As Marcus delved into the specifics of their initiatives, the room became a theater of ideas, where the script of progress was written in terms of sustainable projects, technological advancements, and social programs. Each detail illuminated how the capital injected into the community had become a catalyst for change, fostering an environment where growth wasn't measured solely in financial terms but in the flourishing of human potential.

"Let's talk about the sustainable development projects," Marcus continued, projecting images of solar-powered infrastructure, green spaces, and eco-friendly housing on the screen. "Our commitment to environmental responsibility isn't just about meeting regulatory standards; it's about creating a harmonious coexistence between progress and the planet."

The dialogue in the room shifted seamlessly to technological innovation. Marcus, with the enthusiasm of a visionary, showcased how advancements in technology had not only streamlined processes but had also created employment opportunities and empowered the local population. The room, once filled with the hum of discussion, now resonated with the buzz of possibilities.

"Social equity is not a buzzword for us; it's a guiding principle," Marcus emphasized as he presented initiatives that focused on education, healthcare, and community empowerment.

"Our investments have ensured that the benefits of progress reach every corner of the community, breaking down barriers and fostering a sense of inclusion."

The boardroom, now a theater of inspiration, witnessed a symphony of applause. The investors, moved by the tangible impact of their contributions, recognized that their involvement transcended financial gain; it was about being architects of change, catalysts for a brighter tomorrow.

As the applause subsided, Marcus concluded, "Our success story is not just measured in profit margins, but in the faces of the people who now walk the revitalized streets below us, in the children whose education has become a beacon of hope, and in the collective resilience of a community that refused to be defined by its past."

The room, charged with the energy of accomplishment, echoed with a shared sentiment — the realization that strategic investments, when guided by a vision of holistic progress, had the power to redefine the trajectory of a city and the lives intertwined with its future.

In the midst of the applause, Marcus Turner, a visionary leader with a heart for transformative change, looked out over the cityscape below. The twinkling lights, once dimmed by shadows, now shone brightly, illuminating a path towards a future where investments weren't just financial transactions but pledges to build legacies of enduring progress, unity, and resilience for generations to come.

CHAPTER 25
BUILDING BRIDGES

In the heart of Port-au-Prince, where the transformed cityscape echoed the resilience of the community, a new initiative took root. Sister Marie, recognizing the power of collaboration, convened a gathering of religious leaders, community members, and representatives from different faiths at the interfaith community center.

Sister Marie opened the dialogue, "Our city has witnessed remarkable progress, but now we must focus on building bridges that transcend religious and cultural divides. Let this be a sanctuary where unity is not just a concept but a lived reality."

Bishop Esperanza Ruiz, Sheikh Ahmed Al-Farsi, and Rabbi Miriam Cohen, along with leaders from various faiths, embraced the idea of building bridges. The discussion revolved around how diverse religious communities could come together to contribute to the city's ongoing transformation.

Bishop Ruiz, her compassionate gaze encompassing the room, spoke first, "Our faiths share common values of compassion, justice, and love for our neighbors. Let us find ways to amplify these shared principles and create a city where everyone feels a sense of belonging."

Sheikh Al-Farsi, a symbol of dignity, added, "Education is a powerful tool for dispelling misconceptions. Let us collaborate on programs that promote understanding among the youth, fostering a generation that appreciates the beauty in our diversity."

Rabbi Cohen, her wisdom evident in every word, suggested, "Our religious institutions can collaborate on community projects – building schools, clinics, and spaces for communal gatherings. Together, we can build bridges that go beyond words and manifest in tangible contributions to our shared home."

The leaders, fueled by a collective commitment to unity, outlined specific initiatives. They envisioned joint community events, where members from different faiths could come together to celebrate cultural festivals and religious holidays. The interfaith community center, already a symbol of unity, would become a hub for collaborative projects that transcended religious boundaries.

One of the ambitious projects discussed was the construction of houses of worship that reflected the diversity of faith within the community. A multi faith complex, comprising a church, mosque, synagogue, and spaces for other religious practices, would stand as a testament to the harmonious coexistence of different beliefs.

The leaders recognized the symbolic power of such a complex. It would not only provide spaces for worship but also become a physical manifestation of the city's commitment to religious harmony. Annette, leveraging her connections, secured funding for the project from local businesses and international organizations.

As construction began on the multi faith complex, the leaders engaged in dialogue with their respective communities. They sought input, addressed concerns, and emphasized the shared vision of a city where religious diversity was not just tolerated but embraced.

Another initiative that gained momentum was the introduction of cultural exchange programs. Religious leaders recognized the importance of breaking down cultural barriers and fostering connections among community members.

Sister Marie, drawing from the success of the School of Dreams, proposed expanding cultural exchange programs to include not only students but also adults. Workshops, seminars, and events would create opportunities for individuals from different faiths to engage in meaningful dialogue and collaborative activities.

The leaders, recognizing the transformative potential of these programs, envisioned a city where diversity was not just acknowledged but celebrated. The cultural exchange initiatives became a bridge, connecting hearts and minds across religious lines.

To address societal challenges, the leaders recognized the need for open dialogue on faith and social issues. Bishop Ruiz, Sheikh Al-Farsi, and Rabbi Cohen organized forums where community members could discuss how their faiths addressed issues such as poverty, inequality, and social justice.

These discussions were not about converting or persuading; rather, they aimed to build understanding and find common ground. The leaders encouraged their communities to actively engage in community service projects that addressed the shared values of compassion and justice.

Months later, the multi faith complex stood tall, a testament to the collective efforts of the community. Its inauguration became a momentous occasion, attended by religious leaders, community members, and international guests. The leaders, standing side by side, addressed the gathered crowd.

Bishop Ruiz spoke, "This complex is not just a collection of buildings; it's a living testimony to the harmony that can exist among different faiths. Let it be a reminder that our diversity is not a source of division but a strength that enriches us all."

Sheikh Al-Farsi added, "In this complex, we celebrate the shared values that unite us – values of compassion, justice, and a commitment to the well-being of our community. May it serve as a beacon of unity for generations to come."

Rabbi Cohen, her voice resonant with hope, concluded, "As we open these doors, let us also open our hearts to one another. Together, we have built bridges that span across religious lines, creating a city where every individual, regardless of their faith, feels a sense of belonging."

The leaders, along with community members, entered the complex together. The spaces for worship, adorned with symbols from different faiths, reflected the unity and diversity of the city. The complex became a living testament to the transformative power of building bridges – bridges that connected hearts, minds, and spirits.

As the sun set over the multi faith complex, casting a warm glow on its architectural marvels, the leaders stood together, witnessing the realization of a vision that had started as a dialogue in a community center. The city, now adorned with symbols of unity, embraced a future where faith was not a source of division but a force that brought people together in a tapestry of shared values and collective aspirations.

CHAPTER 26
ANNETTE'S VISION: BEYOND THE TURMOIL

Annette, with a fervent vision for the future, gathered the community leaders, entrepreneurs, and artists in a space where creativity and innovation thrived – the business hub created as part of the economic resurgence.

Annette, her eyes gleaming with determination, opened the dialogue, "We've achieved remarkable progress, but now let's dream even bigger. Beyond the economic revitalization, I see a city that has become a global hub for innovation, arts, and sustainable living. Let's weave a tapestry of progress that transcends the turmoil of the past."

Marcus Turner, intrigued by the prospect, spoke, "The city has the potential to become a hub for technological innovation. Imagine startups, research centers, and incubators creating a vibrant ecosystem that attracts talent from around the world. We can position Port-au-Prince as a city that doesn't just adapt to technology but pioneers it."

Annette nodded, "Exactly, Marcus. Let's invest in innovation districts, where collaboration and creativity flourish. The School of Dreams can be at the center, nurturing the next generation of tech visionaries."

The artists in the room, representing the cultural vibrancy of the city, expressed their enthusiasm for Annette's vision.

One of the muralists, Pablo, shared, "Art has the power to heal, inspire, and connect. Let's create public art installations, galleries, and events that showcase the rich cultural tapestry of our community."

Annette added, "Our city should be a canvas where every corner tells a story. Art not only beautifies but also becomes a catalyst for dialogue and understanding."

Recognizing the importance of environmental stewardship, Annette turned to sustainable living. "Let's lead the way in eco-friendly practices. Green roofs, renewable energy projects, and community gardens can be integrated into our urban planning. Our city can be a model for sustainable living, showcasing that progress doesn't have to come at the expense of our planet."

Sophie Moreau, the passionate educator, suggested, "We can incorporate sustainability education into our schools, teaching the next generation the importance of environmental responsibility."

To celebrate the diversity that defined the city, Annette proposed the creation of annual cultural festivals. "Let's organize events that highlight the music, dance, and traditions of our various communities. These festivals can become not only a source of joy but also economic drivers, attracting visitors from near and far."

President Martine Laurent, appreciating the idea, said, "Cultural exchange is a powerful tool for fostering understanding. Let's invite artists and performers from different parts of the world to showcase their talents here, creating a global dialogue right in our own streets."

Annette, with her global perspective, emphasized the importance of international collaboration.

"Let's forge partnerships with cities known for their innovation and sustainability. We can learn from their experiences and share our unique story of resilience and progress. Port-au-Prince can become a beacon of hope and inspiration for cities facing similar challenges."

Marcus, recognizing the economic potential, added, "International collaboration can also attract foreign investments. Our city, with its renewed identity, can be a destination for businesses seeking to be part of a community-driven, forward-thinking environment."

As the dialogue unfolded, Annette's vision evolved into a comprehensive plan – a blueprint for a city that transcended its past and embraced a future defined by innovation, culture, and sustainability.

In the weeks that followed, the leaders, in collaboration with urban planners, architects, and international consultants, began implementing Annette's vision. Innovation districts sprouted, adorned with cutting-edge buildings that housed tech startups, research centers, and collaborative workspaces.

Art installations adorned public spaces, turning the city into an open-air gallery that celebrated diversity. Sustainable initiatives, from solar-powered streetlights to community gardens, transformed neighborhoods, showcasing that progress and environmental responsibility could go hand in hand.

Cultural festivals became annual highlights, drawing visitors from around the world. The streets resonated with the beats of different music genres, the colors of diverse traditional attire, and the aroma of global cuisines. The city, once defined by turmoil, now embraced a narrative of unity, creativity, and progress.

Annette, during an international conference on sustainable cities, shared Port-au-Prince's journey. "Our city has become a testament to what happens when a community dares to dream beyond the turmoil of its past. We are not just rebuilding; we are redefining what it means to thrive in the face of adversity."

As the city transformed, international attention turned toward Port-au-Prince. Entrepreneurs, artists, and environmentalists found inspiration in its story. The city became a case study, a symbol of how visionary leadership and community collaboration could lead to a renaissance beyond expectations.

One evening, Annette stood on a rooftop overlooking the city, illuminated by the vibrant lights of progress. The business hub below buzzed with activity, the mural-adorned streets told stories of resilience, and the innovative skyline symbolized a future where the city stood as a global beacon of inspiration.

President Martine Laurent, joining Annette on the rooftop, remarked, "Your vision has not only transformed our city but also inspired others to believe in the limitless potential of collective dreams."

Annette, looking out at the city that had become a manifestation of her vision, replied, "This is just the beginning, Martine. Our city's story is a testament to the power of collaboration and the belief that, even in the face of turmoil, we can build a future that transcends expectations."

As they stood together, overlooking the transformed city, Annette's vision had become a reality that radiated far beyond Port-au-Prince – a story of resilience, innovation, and the limitless possibilities that unfold when a community dreams together.

CHAPTER 27
RAYS OF EDUCATION

Dedicated to sculpting a brighter future, leaders convened in the transformed city of Port-au-Prince, their determination echoing through the vibrant streets. This time, the focus was on the heartbeat of progress – education. Sister Marie, Professor Sophie Moreau, and a coalition of educators, philanthropists, and policymakers convened at the newly expanded School of Dreams.

Sister Marie, her eyes reflecting both compassion and hope, addressed the gathering, "Education is the key that unlocks the doors to a brighter future. Let this be a space where every child, regardless of their background, can embrace the rays of knowledge that lead to empowerment and transformation."

Professor Moreau, the passionate educator, shared her vision for expanding the School of Dreams into a comprehensive educational complex. "We have the opportunity to create an environment where students not only excel academically but also explore their passions. Let's introduce specialized programs in arts, sciences, and technology to cater to the diverse talents within our community."

An entrepreneur, inspired by the vision, pledged support, "I'll fund a state-of-the-art science lab to ignite the curiosity of our young minds. The future scientists of Port-au-Prince can start their journeys right here."

Recognizing the importance of a global perspective, the leaders discussed initiatives to connect students with peers from around the world. Annette, leveraging her international networks, proposed, "Let's establish virtual exchange programs where our students can interact with classrooms in different countries. This not only broadens their horizons but fosters a sense of global citizenship."

President Martine Laurent, appreciating the idea, added, "Technology has made the world smaller. Our students should be equipped with the skills and mindset to thrive in an interconnected global society."

To ensure that education was accessible to all, the leaders discussed the implementation of scholarship programs. Marcus Turner, the seasoned investor, suggested, "Let's create a fund that supports students from underprivileged backgrounds. Scholarships for higher education can be a powerful tool for breaking the cycles of poverty and inequality."

Annette, with her financial acumen, said, "I'll reach out to businesses and international organizations to contribute to the scholarship fund. Investing in education is an investment in the future prosperity of our community."

In the multicultural tapestry of Port-au-Prince, the leaders emphasized the importance of cultural education. Bishop Esperanza Ruiz, Sheikh Ahmed Al-Farsi, and Rabbi Miriam Cohen proposed programs that taught students about different religions, fostering tolerance and understanding.

Sister Marie, with a nod, said, "Our students should not only excel academically but also embody the values of empathy and respect. Cultural education is not just about tolerance; it's about celebrating the richness that diversity brings to our community."

The leaders recognized that education extended beyond the classroom walls. Annette suggested, "Let's engage parents and community members in the education process. Workshops, seminars, and programs that involve the whole community will create a supportive ecosystem for our students."

The educators, nodding in agreement, envisioned a city where every individual, from children to adults, saw themselves as lifelong learners actively contributing to the progress of the community.

In the era of technology, the leaders discussed incorporating digital tools into the educational framework. Sophie Moreau proposed, "Let's ensure that every student has access to digital devices and internet connectivity. Technology can bridge gaps and provide equal opportunities for learning."

Marcus, inspired by the idea, offered, "I'll collaborate with tech companies to donate devices and sponsor initiatives that promote digital literacy. Our students should be well-prepared for the opportunities of the digital age."

As the dialogue unfolded, the vision for the School of Dreams expanded into a comprehensive strategy for education in Port-au-Prince – a strategy that aimed not only at academic excellence but also at nurturing well-rounded individuals with a global perspective.

In the months that followed, the School of Dreams underwent a transformative expansion. The science lab became a hub of experimentation and discovery, the classrooms buzzed with discussions on global issues, and scholarship programs opened doors of opportunity for aspiring students.

The virtual exchange programs allowed Port-au-Prince students to connect with peers in different corners of the world. Cultural education initiatives brought the community closer, fostering an environment where diversity was not just acknowledged but celebrated.

The scholarship fund, fueled by contributions from businesses, international organizations, and local philanthropists, supported students as they pursued higher education. The once-narrow pathways to academic success broadened, providing rays of hope to those who dared to dream.

The community, actively engaged in educational programs, became a living testament to the transformative power of education. Parents attended workshops, elders shared their wisdom, and students, inspired by a future of possibilities, took ownership of their learning journeys.

The impact of the education initiatives became evident on graduation day. The School of Dreams, adorned with symbols of achievement, echoed with the cheers of students, families, and community members. Bishop Ruiz, Sheikh Al-Farsi, and Rabbi Cohen, representing different faiths, stood side by side, delivering a message of unity and shared values.

President Martine Laurent, addressing the graduates, said, "Your education is not just a personal achievement; it's a contribution to the collective progress of our community. As you step into the world, carry with you the values of empathy, knowledge, and a commitment to making a positive impact."

Sister Marie, witnessing the graduates who had journeyed through the expanded School of Dreams, felt a profound sense of fulfillment. The rays of education had illuminated not just the minds.

CHAPTER 28
THE MOSQUE ON ELM STREET

The community, fueled by a shared vision of inclusivity, gathered to inaugurate a symbol of harmony – the Mosque on Elm Street. Sheikh Ahmed Al-Farsi, alongside Bishop Esperanza Ruiz and Rabbi Miriam Cohen, stood at the entrance, ready to welcome the community to this transformative space.

The Mosque on Elm Street was not just a place of worship; it was a testament to the city's commitment to unity in diversity. President Martine Laurent, addressing the diverse crowd, said, "This mosque is a celebration of our city's rich tapestry. It represents the harmony that can exist when different faiths come together with a shared commitment to understanding and respect."

Sheikh Ahmed, his voice resonant with gratitude, added, "In Islam, we are taught that diversity is a sign of Allah's greatness. Let this mosque be a symbol of our unity as a community that embraces and celebrates our differences."

Bishop Ruiz, with a gentle smile, said, "Our faiths may differ, but our shared values of compassion, justice, and love for our neighbors bind us together. The Mosque on Elm Street is not just a place for our Muslim brothers and sisters; it's a space for all of us to come together, learn from one another, and grow as a community."

Rabbi Cohen, echoing the sentiment, added, "Interfaith dialogue is not just about conversations; it's about building relationships. Let this mosque be a bridge that connects us, fostering understanding and unity."

The mosque, with its elegant design, seamlessly blended with the architectural diversity of Elm Street. Annette, appreciating the significance of the moment, said, "The beauty of this mosque lies not just in its physical structure but in the message, it sends – that our city thrives when every community is respected and valued."

The architects, inspired by the vision of an inclusive mosque, had incorporated elements that reflected the cultural and architectural heritage of Port-au-Prince. The calligraphy on the walls told stories of unity, and the domed structure stood tall as a symbol of strength and resilience.

The construction of the Mosque on Elm Street was a collaborative effort that involved not only the Muslim community but also individuals from various faiths. Marcus Turner, leveraging his connections in the business community, had facilitated financial support from local businesses and international donors.

Annette, who had played a key role in project management, said, "This mosque is a testament to what we can achieve when we come together with a shared purpose. It's a reflection of the strength that emerges from unity and collaboration."

Inside the mosque, the leaders envisioned educational initiatives that went beyond religious teachings. Professor Sophie Moreau, recognizing the transformative power of education, proposed, "Let's establish programs that promote cultural exchange and understanding.

The Mosque on Elm Street can be a hub for workshops, seminars, and events that bring people together to learn about each other's traditions."

The community members, nodding in agreement, saw the mosque not only as a place of worship but as a center for learning and dialogue.

In the courtyard of the mosque, a community garden took root. Sister Marie, who had been instrumental in fostering community gardens throughout the city, said, "Let this garden be a symbol of our shared responsibility for the earth. It's a space where the community can come together, tend to the land, and share moments of reflection and camaraderie."

Gathering spaces, adorned with benches and artistic installations, became places for people of different faiths to sit together, engage in conversations, and build connections that transcended religious boundaries.

As part of the mosque's commitment to interfaith harmony, the leaders organized celebrations that brought together members of different faiths. Festivals, community meals, and cultural events became opportunities for individuals to experience the richness of each other's traditions.

Rabbi Cohen, participating in one of the interfaith celebrations, remarked, "The Mosque on Elm Street has become a living example of what happens when people choose to focus on what unites them rather than what divides them. It's a beacon of hope for cities around the world."

Recognizing the importance of engaging the youth, the leaders established programs within the mosque that catered to the younger generation.

Sheikh Ahmed, addressing a group of enthusiastic teenagers, said, "This mosque is your space. It's a place for you to learn, grow, and contribute to the betterment of our community. Your ideas and energy are integral to the success of this endeavor."

The youth, inspired by the inclusive environment of the Mosque on Elm Street, actively participated in educational programs, community service initiatives, and cultural exchanges.

Months after the inauguration, the doors of the Mosque on Elm Street remained open not just to the Muslim community but to everyone. Annette, during a community gathering, emphasized, "This mosque is a symbol of our commitment to inclusivity. It's a space where people of all faiths, backgrounds, and beliefs can come together in a spirit of unity and friendship."

The mosque became a venue for art exhibitions, musical performances, and community forums. The leaders, standing together in the courtyard, witnessed a city that embraced diversity within its borders.

As the years passed, the Mosque on Elm Street became an integral part of the city's identity. It stood not only as a place of worship but as a living testament to the power of unity, understanding, and shared values.

Bishop Ruiz, Sheikh Ahmed Al-Farsi, and Rabbi Cohen, their friendship deepening through years of collaboration, stood together as a symbol of interfaith harmony. The community garden flourished, the gathering spaces buzzed with conversations, and the educational programs continued to inspire individuals of all ages.

Annette, reflecting on the journey, said, "The Mosque on Elm Street is not just a building; it's a legacy of harmony that we leave for future generations.

It's a reminder that, in embracing our differences, we build a city that stands as a beacon of unity and respect."

As the sun set over Elm Street, casting a warm glow on the mosque and its surroundings, the leaders, community members, and individuals from various faiths stood together in a moment of shared gratitude. The Mosque on Elm Street had become a living legacy – a testament to the city's commitment to a future where diversity was not only accepted but celebrated, and where places of worship became symbols of unity that transcended the confines of their walls.

CHAPTER 29
UNRAVELING DISASTER

Amidst the tranquil backdrop of Port-au-Prince's bustling streets, a tranquil morning was shattered by the unrelenting force of nature. It was a day much like any other, with residents going about their daily routines, unaware of the impending calamity that would soon descend upon their city.

The atmosphere was charged with a sense of foreboding as dark clouds gathered ominously overhead, casting a shadow over the vibrant city below. The first signs of the impending disaster came in the form of distant rumblings, like the growls of a restless beast stirring from slumber.

As the morning wore on, the rumblings grew louder, accompanied by flashes of lightning that streaked across the sky like fiery serpents. The residents of Port-au-Prince looked on with trepidation, their hearts gripped with a sense of fear and uncertainty.

Then, without warning, disaster struck. The heavens opened up, unleashing a torrential downpour that pounded the city with relentless fury. The streets quickly turned into raging rivers, swallowing everything in their path as they surged forward with unstoppable force.

The once-tranquil neighborhoods of Port-au-Prince were transformed into scenes of chaos and devastation. Homes were swept away like flimsy cardboard boxes, their frail structures no match for the wrath of the raging floodwaters.

The city's infrastructure crumbled under the onslaught, with roads collapsing and bridges buckling under the weight of the deluge. Power lines snapped like twigs, plunging entire neighborhoods into darkness as the electrical grid faltered and failed.

Amidst the chaos, the residents of Port-au-Prince found themselves trapped in a nightmare from which there seemed to be no escape. Many sought refuge on rooftops, clinging desperately to whatever semblance of safety they could find as the floodwaters continued to rise inexorably around them.

For hours that felt like an eternity, the city was gripped by a sense of despair and helplessness as the disaster unfolded with merciless efficiency. It was a cataclysm of unprecedented proportions, one that would leave an indelible mark on the collective psyche of Port-au-Prince for generations to come.

And yet, amidst the chaos and devastation, there were glimmers of hope and resilience. Neighbors reached out to help one another, offering whatever assistance they could to those in need. Strangers became allies in the fight for survival, united by a common bond forged in the crucible of adversity.

As the waters began to recede and the storm clouds finally dispersed, the true extent of the devastation became painfully clear. Entire neighborhoods lay in ruins, their once-proud buildings reduced to rubble and debris. The cityscape was transformed into a landscape of desolation, with the scars of the disaster serving as a grim reminder of the fragility of human existence in the face of nature's fury.

In the aftermath of the catastrophe, the residents of Port-au-Prince were left to pick up the pieces of their shattered lives and rebuild from the ruins.

It was a daunting task, one that would require courage, resilience, and unwavering determination.

But amidst the wreckage and despair, there was also a glimmer of hope – a belief that, together, they could overcome even the greatest of challenges and emerge stronger on the other side. And so, with hearts heavy with grief but spirits buoyed by hope, the people of Port-au-Prince began the long and arduous journey of rebuilding their beloved city from the ruins of disaster.

CHAPTER 30
HARMONY AMIDST CHAOS

In the heart of Port-au-Prince, a city that had weathered storms and challenges, a group of leaders convened in the aftermath of a devastating natural disaster. The once-vibrant neighborhood, now marked by chaos and destruction, served as the backdrop for a crucial meeting. President Martine Laurent, flanked by community leaders, environmental experts, and empathetic visionaries, stood at the center of a makeshift gathering space.

The air was heavy with the scent of debris and the echoes of sorrow. The leaders, looking out at the ravaged streets, recognized the enormity of the task ahead. Bishop Esperanza Ruiz, her gaze fixed on the damaged church, spoke with a somber tone, "Our community is resilient, but the impact of this disaster is substantial. We must come together, not just as leaders but as neighbors, to rebuild what was lost."

Sheikh Ahmed Al-Farsi, his eyes reflecting the pain of the community, added, "In the face of adversity, we find strength in our unity. Let this moment be a catalyst for collective action and compassion."

As the leaders assessed the immediate needs of the community, Sister Marie, known for her dedication to humanitarian efforts, proposed a plan for immediate relief. "Our first priority is to provide shelter, food, and medical assistance to those affected. Let's mobilize volunteers, reach out to aid organizations, and ensure that no one in our community is left without support."

Marcus Turner, leveraging his expertise in logistics, is committed to organizing the distribution of resources. "We need a coordinated effort to ensure that aid reaches every corner of the neighborhood. Timely and efficient relief can make a significant difference in alleviating the immediate hardships our community faces."

Recognizing the recurring challenges posed by natural disasters, Professor Sophie Moreau emphasized the importance of environmental resilience in reconstruction efforts. "Let's consider sustainable practices in rebuilding. Green infrastructure, resilient construction materials, and urban planning that takes into account the environmental vulnerabilities of our region can pave the way for a more resilient future."

Annette, with her strategic mindset, saw an opportunity to collaborate with environmental organizations. "By incorporating environmental considerations into our rebuilding efforts, we not only protect our community from future disasters but also contribute to a global movement for sustainable urban development."

The ruins of cultural landmarks raised concerns about the preservation of the community's identity. Rabbi Miriam Cohen, pointing towards the damaged synagogue, said, "Our cultural heritage is intertwined with the strength of our community. Let's prioritize the restoration of our cultural landmarks, ensuring that the symbols of our identity remain standing."

Bishop Ruiz, gesturing towards the church, added, "In rebuilding, let's not just restore buildings; let's revive the spirit of our community. Our cultural spaces are not just structures; they are repositories of our shared history and resilience."

The trauma experienced by the community members called for a holistic approach to rebuilding. President Martine, acknowledging the emotional toll, emphasized the need for psychosocial support. "Let's collaborate with mental health professionals, community leaders, and support groups to provide emotional assistance to those who have endured the trauma of this disaster."

Sister Marie, who had been a pillar of support in previous crises, committed to organizing community gatherings and counseling sessions. "Healing is a collective journey. By fostering a sense of community and providing emotional support, we can help our neighbors navigate the difficult path ahead."

To ensure that the rebuilding efforts reflected the aspirations of the community, the leaders initiated inclusive decision-making processes. Sheikh Ahmed, his commitment to inclusivity unwavering, said, "Every member of our community should have a voice in the rebuilding process. Let's organize town hall meetings, engage in open dialogue, and consider the diverse perspectives that make our community strong."

Annette, known for her dedication to community engagement, suggested, "We can create committees that include representatives from different sectors – residents, business owners, educators. This collaborative approach will not only ensure inclusivity but also lead to more effective and sustainable solutions."

Recognizing the resilience and potential of the youth, the leaders discussed initiatives to empower the younger generation. Professor Sophie Moreau proposed educational programs, skill development workshops, and mentorship opportunities. "Our youth are the future architects of our community.

By investing in their education and providing them with the tools to rebuild, we are laying the foundation for a more resilient and vibrant future."

The youth, represented by enthusiastic individuals, expressed their commitment to actively participate in the rebuilding process. "This is our community, and we are ready to contribute our skills, energy, and ideas to rebuild and strengthen it," declared a young community leader.

As the leaders brainstormed strategies for rebuilding, President Martine addressed the gathering with a message of hope and determination. "This crisis has tested our community, but let it also be the catalyst for unity, compassion, and transformation. In our collective response, we will find the strength to rebuild not just structures but the very fabric of our community."

Bishop Ruiz, Sheikh Ahmed Al-Farsi, and Rabbi Cohen, representing different faiths, stood together in a symbolic gesture of unity. The community members, inspired by the leaders' commitment, joined hands in a circle – a symbol of solidarity and resilience.

In the weeks and months that followed, the leaders, community members, and volunteers worked tirelessly to implement the comprehensive rebuilding plan. Immediate relief efforts provided comfort to those in need, environmental considerations shaped resilient infrastructure, and cultural preservation initiatives breathed life into the symbols of the community's identity.

Town hall meetings became forums for open dialogue, where diverse voices contributed to the decision-making process. The youth, actively engaged in educational and skill development programs, became ambassadors of positive change.

As the community gardens flourished, gathering spaces buzzed with renewed energy, and cultural landmarks stood tall once again, the neighborhood underwent a journey of renewal. The scars of the disaster became testaments to the community's strength, and the leaders, united in purpose, witnessed a transformation that went beyond physical reconstruction.

One day, as the sun rose over the revitalized neighborhood, President Martine, standing amidst the rebuilt structures and vibrant community spaces, addressed the gathering. "Today marks not just a new chapter but a testament to our resilience and unity. We have faced challenges, rebuilt what was lost, and emerged stronger as a community."

Bishop Ruiz, Sheikh Ahmed Al-Farsi, and Rabbi Cohen, standing alongside President Martine, shared a moment of reflection. The Mosque on Elm Street, the cultural landmarks, and the environmentally resilient infrastructure stood as symbols of a community that had found harmony amidst chaos.

As the leaders, community members, and youth celebrated the journey of renewal, a sense of pride and optimism filled the air. The disaster had tested their mettle, but the response had demonstrated the power of unity, compassion, and shared vision. The neighborhood, once marked by chaos, had become a beacon of resilience and hope – a living testament to the strength that emerges when a community stands together in the face of adversity.

CHAPTER 31
RESILIENCE IN THE RUINS

In the heart of Port-au-Prince, where the scars of the past were still visible, a group of community leaders, architects, and urban planners gathered amidst the remnants of what was once a vibrant neighborhood. The ruins stood as a testament to the resilience of a community that had weathered storms, both natural and man-made.

President Martine Laurent, her eyes fixed on the remnants of a once-thriving marketplace, spoke with a solemn yet determined tone, "This place holds memories of both hardship and strength. Today, we stand not just amidst ruins but in the crucible of our collective resilience. Let's envision a renewal that rises from the ashes, a testament to our unwavering spirit."

Sister Marie, the embodiment of compassion, turned to the gathered community members and said, "Your stories, your experiences – they are the foundation upon which we'll rebuild. Let this not be a top-down reconstruction but a collaborative effort that honors the voices of the community."

A local artist, surveying the broken walls that once showcased murals of hope, added, "The art that adorned these streets told our story. Let's rebuild not just with bricks but with the vibrant colors of our resilience."

The architects and urban planners, armed with blueprints and maps, outlined a holistic approach to reconstruction.

Annette, with her strategic mindset, suggested, "Let's not just rebuild structures; let's create spaces that serve the needs of the community. Green spaces, community centers, and affordable housing should be woven into the fabric of the reconstruction plan."

Marcus Turner, considering the economic impact, added, "We can leverage this opportunity to create job opportunities. Local businesses should play a pivotal role in the reconstruction, ensuring that the economic benefits are shared among the community members."

Amidst the ruins, remnants of cultural landmarks stood as silent witnesses to the city's history. Bishop Esperanza Ruiz, advocating for the preservation of cultural heritage, said, "Our churches, temples, and mosques are not just buildings; they are symbols of our identity. Let's rebuild with a commitment to preserving our cultural heritage."

Sheikh Ahmed Al-Farsi and Rabbi Miriam Cohen echoed the sentiment, emphasizing the importance of unity in the reconstruction efforts. "In rebuilding, let's create spaces that foster understanding and respect among different faiths," Rabbi Cohen proposed.

The city, scarred by previous disasters, now had an opportunity to rebuild with sustainability in mind. Professor Sophie Moreau, passionate about environmental stewardship, suggested, "Green building practices, renewable energy, and water conservation should be integral to the reconstruction plan. Let's create a city that not only survives but thrives in harmony with nature."

The architects nodded, incorporating sustainability into their designs, envisioning a city that not only rose from the ruins but also set an example for future urban development.

Recognizing the importance of inclusivity, President Martine addressed the gathered leaders, "Every decision we make in this reconstruction process should be inclusive. We must actively seek the input of those who call this community home – the ones who have endured the trials and triumphs of life amidst these ruins."

Community workshops were organized, inviting residents to share their visions for the future. The elders spoke of traditions that should be preserved, the youth shared dreams of modern amenities, and families emphasized the need for safety and security.

As the reconstruction plan took shape, the leaders proposed the creation of symbolic structures that would serve as beacons of hope. Annette suggested, "Let's build a memorial that honors the resilience of our community. A place where future generations can come to understand the challenges we faced and the strength with which we rose above them."

A local poet, capturing the collective sentiment, proposed the creation of a community library. "In the midst of ruins, let's build a space that nurtures the minds of our children. A library that becomes a sanctuary of knowledge, a symbol of our commitment to a brighter future."

The reconstruction efforts, fueled by community engagement, unfolded with a spirit of determination. Construction sites buzzed with activity, and the sounds of hammers and drills echoed through the streets that were slowly being resurrected.

Annette, leveraging her connections, secured funding from international organizations committed to resilient urban development. The community members, actively participating in the rebuilding process, felt a sense of ownership in the transformation of their neighborhood.

Months later, as the first structures of the reconstructed neighborhood took shape, a celebration was organized. The community members, alongside the leaders, gathered in what was now a vibrant square adorned with murals depicting the journey from ruins to resilience.

Sister Marie, addressing the crowd, said, "Look around – this is not just a physical reconstruction. It's a testament to the strength that arises when a community comes together. In every brick laid and every mural painted, we see the indomitable spirit of Port-au-Prince."

The symbolic structures, the memorial, and the community library were unveiled on a day that marked the beginning of a new chapter. President Martine Laurent, standing amidst the reconstructed marketplace, addressed the gathered crowd, "Today, we inaugurate not just buildings but symbols of hope, resilience, and the unbreakable spirit of our community."

The memorial, with its inscription of shared struggles and triumphs, became a place for reflection and remembrance. The community library, filled with books donated by local authors and international contributors, opened its doors to eager readers.

As the sun set over the reconstructed neighborhood, casting a warm glow on the revitalized streets, the leaders stood together. The ruins that had once symbolized destruction now bore witness to a community that had not just survived but had emerged stronger.

Bishop Ruiz, Sheikh Al-Farsi, and Rabbi Cohen, representing different faiths, offered prayers for the future. The local poet recited verses that celebrated the journey from desolation to determination. Annette, looking at the transformed neighborhood, remarked, "This is not just a reconstruction; it's a legacy of resilience that will echo through generations."

The community members, now living amidst structures that embodied their collective strength, felt a renewed sense of pride. The reconstructed neighborhood, with its sustainable practices, inclusive spaces, and symbolic structures, became a model for other communities facing similar challenges.

President Martine Laurent, with a sense of accomplishment, said, "Port-au-Prince has not just rebuilt; it has shown the world what it means to build back better. Our story is not one of the ruins; it's a narrative of resilience, hope, and the enduring spirit of a community that refuses to be defined by its challenges."

As the leaders, community members, and children played amidst the revitalized marketplace, the echoes of laughter mingled with the gentle breeze. The reconstructed neighborhood, once marked by ruins, now stood as a living testament to the triumph of resilience over adversity – a story that would inspire cities around the world to envision a future beyond the scars of the past.

CHAPTER 32
MARCUS'S INVESTMENTS: SEEDS OF CHANGE

Marcus Turner, the seasoned investor known for his strategic vision, found himself standing at the intersection of opportunity and community need. The recent disasters had left scars on the city, but Marcus saw beyond the devastation. With a deep sense of commitment and a desire to catalyze change, he embarked on a journey to sow seeds of transformation through strategic investments.

Amidst the remnants of the once-thriving marketplace, Marcus convened a meeting with local entrepreneurs, community leaders, and economic experts. The air was charged with a mix of hope and uncertainty as the group gathered to discuss the potential for rebuilding the economic backbone of the community.

President Martine Laurent, acknowledging Marcus's expertise, said, "Our community needs more than just reconstruction; we need economic revitalization. Marcus, your insights can be the key to unlocking opportunities that will empower our local businesses and create sustainable growth."

Marcus, nodding in agreement, replied, "Rebuilding the economy is not just about attracting external investments; it's about empowering the existing businesses, fostering entrepreneurship, and ensuring that the economic growth is inclusive."

One of Marcus's first initiatives was to identify and support local businesses that had the potential to thrive with the right investment. He met with entrepreneurs like Jeanne Baptiste, the owner of a family-run bakery that had been a neighborhood staple for generations.

Sitting across from Jeanne, Marcus said, "Your bakery is more than a business; it's a part of the community's identity. With the right support, we can not only rebuild what was lost but also create a foundation for sustained growth. Let's discuss how we can enhance your operations, expand your reach, and contribute to the economic resurgence of our community."

Jeanne, inspired by Marcus's commitment, shared her aspirations for the bakery. "I've always dreamed of modernizing our equipment, introducing new products, and reaching a wider audience. With your guidance, Marcus, I believe we can turn this dream into a reality."

To foster a culture of entrepreneurship, Marcus proposed the establishment of an entrepreneurial incubator – a space where aspiring business owners could receive mentorship, access to resources, and opportunities to transform their ideas into viable enterprises.

Marcus met with young entrepreneurs like Pierre Desrosiers, who had a vision for a sustainable fashion brand that celebrated the cultural heritage of Port-au-Prince. "Your idea is not just a business; it's a reflection of our community's rich history. Through the entrepreneurial incubator, we can provide you with the support needed to turn this vision into a thriving venture," Marcus assured Pierre.

Pierre, excited by the prospect, replied, "With the right mentorship and resources, I believe we can create a brand that not only contributes to the local economy but also becomes a symbol of our resilience and creativity."

As Marcus explored opportunities, he recognized the potential for revitalizing commercial spaces that had been vacant or underutilized. He met with building owners, architects, and urban planners to discuss ways to breathe new life into these spaces, creating hubs of economic activity.

Annette, with her strategic mindset, suggested, "Let's reimagine these spaces as community hubs – places where local businesses, artists, and entrepreneurs can come together. By infusing energy into these areas, we not only enhance the visual appeal of our neighborhood but also create economic nodes that benefit everyone."

Marcus, aligning with the vision, added, "Revitalizing commercial spaces is not just about attracting customers; it's about creating a sense of community, encouraging collaboration, and fostering a vibrant local economy."

Marcus, known for his commitment to sustainable investments, explored opportunities in renewable energy, eco-friendly practices, and green infrastructure. He met with environmental experts, architects, and representatives from local organizations to discuss ways to integrate sustainability into the economic revitalization efforts.

Sophie Moreau, the passionate educator with a keen interest in environmental stewardship, joined the conversation. "Our rebuilding efforts provide a unique opportunity to embrace sustainable practices.

By investing in renewable energy, green construction, and environmentally conscious businesses, we not only create a more resilient community but also contribute to the global movement for sustainable development."

Marcus, recognizing the economic and environmental benefits, pledged to incorporate sustainability into every facet of his investment strategy. "Sustainable investments are not just about protecting the environment; they are about building a future where our community thrives in harmony with nature."

Understanding the importance of a skilled and empowered workforce, Marcus initiated programs for job training, skill development, and education. He collaborated with local schools, vocational training centers, and businesses to create pathways for individuals to acquire the skills needed for emerging job opportunities.

Marcus met with individuals like Marie Chantal, a young woman with a passion for technology but limited access to educational resources. "Your commitment to skill development is inspiring, Marcus. With the right training, I believe I can contribute to the growing tech industry in our city," Marie Chantal expressed.

Encouraged by her enthusiasm, Marcus replied, "Your potential is not defined by your current circumstances. Through our skill development programs, we aim to create opportunities for individuals like you to thrive and contribute to the evolving economic landscape of Port-au-Prince."

To ensure that the benefits of economic revitalization reached every corner of the community, Marcus proposed the creation of a community investment fund. This fund would pool resources from local businesses, investors, and external partners to support initiatives that directly benefit the community.

Annette, recognizing the potential impact, said, "The community investment fund can serve as a catalyst for grassroots projects, community-led initiatives, and social enterprises. By involving the community in decision-making and resource allocation, we empower individuals to actively shape the economic landscape of their neighborhood."

Marcus, committed to the idea of shared prosperity, pledged to contribute a significant portion of his investments to the community fund. "Our success should be measured not just in financial terms but in the positive impact we create within our community. The community investment fund is a vehicle through which we can collectively drive change and build a future that benefits everyone."

As Marcus's investments took root, the neighborhood began to witness a transformation. The local bakery expanded its operations, becoming a hub for community gatherings and cultural celebrations. Pierre's sustainable fashion brand gained recognition not only for its unique designs but also for its commitment to ethical and eco-friendly practices.

The revitalized commercial spaces buzzed with activity, hosting a diverse range of businesses – from artisanal cafes to innovative startups. The entrepreneurial incubator became a breeding ground for creativity, fostering a new generation of business owners who were not only economically successful but also deeply connected to the community.

The community investment fund, fueled by Marcus's initial contributions and the support of local businesses, became a driving force behind grassroots projects. Community gardens flourished, educational programs expanded, and initiatives for environmental resilience gained momentum.

One day, as the community gathered to celebrate the success of Marcus's investments, President Martine spoke with gratitude, "Marcus, your commitment to our community has not only revitalized our economy but has also sown seeds of lasting change. Through your strategic investments, you have empowered local businesses, nurtured entrepreneurship, and created pathways for individuals to thrive."

Marcus, surrounded by entrepreneurs, community leaders, and individuals who had directly benefited from the economic revitalization, humbly replied, "This success is not mine alone; it belongs to the entire community. Together, we have shown that strategic investments, when guided by a vision of inclusivity and sustainability, can be a powerful force for positive change."

As the community members shared stories of their journeys – from challenges to triumphs – Marcus looked around, witnessing a neighborhood that had not only rebuilt but had emerged stronger, more vibrant, and deeply connected. The seeds of change he had planted had grown into a garden of transformation, symbolizing the resilience, creativity, and shared prosperity of Port-au-Prince.

CHAPTER 33
HAITI'S RISING

In the wake of unprecedented challenges, the heart of Port-au-Prince beat with a renewed sense of hope and determination. The leaders, community members, and visionaries who had stood together through crises and triumphs now found themselves at a pivotal moment – the dawn of a new era for Haiti.

As the sun painted the sky in hues of gold, President Martine Laurent stood before a crowd gathered at the reconstructed town square. The once desolate space now teemed with life – a testament to the resilience of the people and the collective efforts that had gone into rebuilding.

"Ladies and gentlemen, today we stand not just on the reconstructed ground but on the foundation of our shared resilience," President Martine declared. "Our journey has been one of rebuilding not just structures but lives, dreams, and the very fabric of our community."

Bishop Esperanza Ruiz, Sheikh Ahmed Al-Farsi, and Rabbi Miriam Cohen, representing the unity of faiths, joined President Martine on the makeshift stage. Together, they symbolized the interfaith harmony that had been a guiding light throughout the rebuilding process.

The newly rebuilt Sister Marie's School of Dreams stood as a beacon of education and possibility.

Professor Sophie Moreau, standing in front of the school, expressed her conviction in the transformative power of education. "In the corridors of this school, the future leaders of Haiti are being nurtured. Education is not just a tool; it's a catalyst for change and empowerment."

The youth, now equipped with skills and knowledge, actively participated in shaping the future of their community. Jean-Claude Desmarais, the renowned economist, noted, "Investing in education is an investment in the very foundation of our nation's prosperity. The seeds we plant in young minds today will blossom into the leaders of tomorrow."

Marcus Turner, whose strategic investments had breathed life into local businesses, stood beside Annette as they surveyed the vibrant marketplace. "This marketplace is not just a center for commerce; it's a symbol of economic resurgence. By investing in our local businesses, we have created a sustainable economic ecosystem that benefits everyone," Marcus remarked.

Annette added, "Our community investment fund has become a driving force for grassroots initiatives. From community gardens to cultural celebrations, we are witnessing the transformative power of collective investment in our shared future."

The Mosque on Elm Street, standing tall with its doors open to all, exemplified the spirit of interfaith harmony. Sheikh Ahmed, Bishop Ruiz, and Rabbi Cohen, standing together, addressed the crowd. "In the embrace of our diverse faiths, we have found strength and unity. The Mosque on Elm Street is a living example of how different beliefs can come together to build a harmonious community," Rabbi Cohen declared.

The mosque had become a hub for interfaith celebrations, cultural events, and educational programs that fostered understanding and respect among different religious communities. It symbolized a shared space where people, regardless of their faith, could come together in the spirit of unity.

Cultural landmarks, once damaged, now stood as resilient symbols of the community's identity. Annette, a driving force behind the cultural revitalization efforts, spoke about the significance of preserving the city's heritage. "Our cultural landmarks are not just structures; they are living narratives of our history and strength. By preserving and celebrating our heritage, we anchor ourselves in the roots that define us."

The community, enriched by cultural celebrations and artistic expressions, embraced the diversity that made Port-au-Prince unique. The streets echoed with the sounds of music, laughter, and the vibrant colors of local art.

The commitment to sustainability echoed in every corner of the rebuilt city. Parks adorned with greenery, eco-friendly buildings, and community gardens showcased the city's dedication to environmental stewardship. Professor Sophie Moreau, an advocate for sustainable practices, emphasized the long-term impact of these efforts.

"Our city is not just rebuilt; it's reimagined. By integrating sustainability into our urban planning and daily practices, we are ensuring a future where our environment thrives alongside our community," Sophie remarked.

Threads of Hope, an initiative that fostered dialogue and understanding among community members, had become a bridge that connected people from different backgrounds.

The dialogue sessions, facilitated by leaders and community volunteers, encouraged open conversations about the challenges and aspirations of individuals.

Annette, reflecting on the success of Threads of Hope, said, "In understanding each other's stories, we break down barriers and build connections. The conversations we have had through Threads of Hope are the threads that weave the fabric of our united community."

As President Martine addressed the crowd in the revitalized town square, she captured the essence of Haiti's rising. "We are not just a city rebuilt; we are a united city – a testament to the power of collaboration, resilience, and shared vision. The challenges we faced did not break us; they forged us into a community that stands tall, proud, and stronger than ever before."

The leaders, community members, and individuals who had played pivotal roles in Haiti's journey of renewal stood together on the stage. Each face reflected the spirit of determination and hope that had propelled the community forward.

As the sun sets over the rejuvenated city, casting a warm glow on its resilient streets, the leaders and community members gathered for a moment of reflection. Annette, Marcus, Professor Sophie, Jean-Claude, Sheikh Ahmed, Bishop Ruiz, Rabbi Cohen, and President Martine – a diverse ensemble united by a common purpose – shared a sense of pride in what they had collectively achieved. President Martine, looking out at the city she served, said, "Our journey does not end here; it evolves. The rising sun today marks the promise of a future where Haiti continues to thrive, innovate, and stand as a beacon of hope for communities around the world."

The community members, representing the strength of Haiti's people, embraced the future with a shared commitment to resilience, unity, and the belief that, in the face of adversity, they had not just survived; they had risen. Haiti's rising was not just a chapter in its history; it was a story of triumph, a testament to the indomitable spirit of a community that had faced challenges and emerged stronger, more vibrant, and more connected than ever before.

CHAPTER 34
SOWING PROSPERITY

The air was infused with the scent of blooming flowers and the energy of a city that had not only rebuilt itself but was now poised for prosperity. Annette, Marcus, Professor Sophie, Jean-Claude, Sheikh Ahmed, Bishop Ruiz, Rabbi Cohen, and President Martine convened to discuss the next phase of their journey – the sowing of prosperity.

In the community garden, Annette articulated her vision for the future. "Our journey of renewal has brought us to a point where we are not just rebuilding but sowing the seeds of prosperity. The community garden is a symbol of growth, sustainability, and the potential for a bountiful future."

The garden, once a patch of desolation, now thrived with a variety of fruits, vegetables, and vibrant flowers.

Annette continued, "Just as we nurture this garden, we will nurture our economy, education, and the overall well-being of our community. It's time to harness the seeds of change we planted and cultivate prosperity for generations to come."

Marcus, the strategic investor whose initiatives had breathed life into local businesses, spoke about the economic landscape. "Our local businesses are the backbone of our community's prosperity. By empowering entrepreneurs, fostering innovation, and creating opportunities for sustainable growth, we can ensure economic prosperity that reaches every corner of Port-au-Prince."

Annette added, "The community investment fund we established is a testament to our commitment to shared prosperity. By reinvesting in local businesses and supporting new ventures, we amplify the impact of our collective efforts."

Professor Sophie, standing amidst the thriving Sister Marie's School of Dreams, emphasized the role of education in sowing the seeds of prosperity. "Education is the foundation on which prosperity is built. By enriching the minds of our youth, providing them with diverse opportunities, and instilling a love for learning, we create a generation equipped to navigate the challenges of the future."

Jean-Claude Desmarais, the renowned economist, spoke about the synergy between education and economic growth. "A well-educated workforce is an asset to our community. Let's continue to invest in educational initiatives that prepare our youth for the evolving landscape of the global economy."

In the shadow of eco-friendly buildings and green spaces, Professor Sophie highlighted the importance of sustainability. "Our commitment to green initiatives is not just an environmental choice; it's an investment in the long-term prosperity of our community. By embracing sustainable practices, we ensure that our city continues to thrive for generations to come."

Marcus, with his focus on sustainable investments, added, "Sustainability is not just a buzzword; it's a strategic choice that aligns economic growth with environmental responsibility. Our initiatives should serve as a model for communities worldwide, showcasing that prosperity and sustainability can go hand in hand."

Sheikh Ahmed, Bishop Ruiz, and Rabbi Cohen, representing the interfaith harmony that had become a hallmark of the community, shared their perspectives on fostering unity and understanding. "In sowing the seeds of prosperity, we must recognize the richness that diversity brings," said Sheikh Ahmed. "Interfaith collaboration is not just about tolerance; it's about celebrating our differences and working together for the common good."

Bishop Ruiz, nodding in agreement, added, "The strength of our community lies in our unity. Let's continue to build bridges between faiths, fostering dialogue and collaboration that transcends religious boundaries."

Rabbi Cohen, looking at the restored synagogue and other cultural landmarks, spoke about the importance of preserving cultural heritage. "Our cultural identity is a source of strength and resilience. As we sow the seeds of prosperity, let's ensure that our rich history and traditions are not just preserved but celebrated."

Annette, passionate about cultural revitalization, shared her thoughts. "Cultural heritage is not just a relic of the past; it's a living expression of who we are. By incorporating our traditions into the fabric of our community, we ensure that prosperity is rooted in the very essence of our identity."

President Martine, standing amidst the revitalized town square, addressed the importance of community engagement. "Prosperity is not a solitary pursuit; it's a collective endeavor that requires the active participation of every member of our community. Let's continue to engage, listen, and involve ourselves in the decisions that shape our shared future."

Annette, known for her community-focused approach, added, "Our community members are the architects of their prosperity. By involving them in decision-making, we empower individuals to contribute to the ongoing development of our city."

Recognizing the potential of youth, Professor Sophie proposed initiatives for youth empowerment. "Our youth are not just the future; they are the present architects of change. By providing them with opportunities for leadership, mentorship, and skill development, we sow the seeds of a vibrant and dynamic future."

Jean-Claude, echoing the sentiment, said, "Youth empowerment is not just an investment in the next generation; it's an investment in the continued prosperity of our community. Let's create pathways for the youth to actively contribute to the shaping of our city."

As the leaders discussed their respective areas of focus, a sense of shared purpose and collaboration filled the air. Annette, summarizing the collective vision, said, "In sowing the seeds of prosperity, we recognize that each facet – education, economy, sustainability, interfaith harmony, cultural preservation, community engagement, and youth empowerment – is interconnected. Our success lies in the synergy of these efforts."

The leaders, with a renewed commitment to their shared vision, stood together at the center of the thriving town square. President Martine, looking at the vibrant community around them, declared, "Our journey continues, and the seeds we sow today will yield a harvest of prosperity that extends far beyond our horizons."

The community members, aware of the collective efforts underway, embraced the vision of a future where Haiti's prosperity would be a beacon of hope and inspiration. As the sun dipped below the horizon, casting a warm glow over the city, the leaders and community members alike felt a profound sense of anticipation for the bountiful harvest that awaited – a future where prosperity flourished, and the resilient spirit of Haiti continued to rise.

CHAPTER 35
RISING FROM ASHES

The dawn of a new day cast its gentle light over Port-au-Prince, illuminating the city's rejuvenated skyline. Annette, Marcus, Professor Sophie, Jean-Claude, Sheikh Ahmed, Bishop Ruiz, Rabbi Cohen, and President Martine gathered in a symbolic circle at the center of the revitalized town square. Their faces reflected on the journey they had undertaken – a journey of rebuilding, unity, and now, the promise of prosperity.

President Martine, standing amidst the bustling marketplace, began the dialogue. "As we stand here today, I cannot help but reflect on the journey we embarked upon. From the ashes of adversity, we rose, not as individuals, but as a united community determined to shape its destiny."

Annette, the visionary behind the cultural revitalization efforts, added, "Our journey wasn't just about rebuilding structures; it was about revitalizing our cultural identity. The landmarks that once stood as remnants now breathe with the vibrancy of our shared history."

Marcus spoke about economic transformation. "The marketplace, once a symbol of desolation, now teems with life. Our investments in local businesses, the entrepreneurial incubator, and sustainable initiatives have not just revitalized the economy but have sown the seeds of lasting prosperity."

Jean-Claude, the renowned economist, chimed in, "Economic growth is not just about numbers; it's about improving the quality of life for every member of our community. By creating opportunities for employment, fostering innovation, and ensuring inclusive growth, we've laid a foundation for sustained prosperity."

Professor Sophie, standing near Sister Marie's School of Dreams, spoke passionately about the role of education. "Our school is not just a structure; it's a sanctuary of learning. The seeds we've planted in the minds of our youth will germinate into a future where education is the key to unlocking endless possibilities."

Annette, nodding in agreement, added, "Education is the cornerstone of prosperity. By nurturing curious minds and providing avenues for skill development, we've empowered our youth to be architects of their own success."

Bishop Ruiz, Sheikh Ahmed, and Rabbi Cohen, standing near the Mosque on Elm Street, reflected on the journey of interfaith collaboration. "Our unity has been a beacon of hope for all," said Sheikh Ahmed. "In a world often divided, our city stands as a testament to the power of harmony among different faiths."

Rabbi Cohen emphasized, "The Mosque on Elm Street has become a symbol of coexistence. It's not just a place of worship; it's a space where diverse communities come together to celebrate our shared humanity."

Annette, surrounded by the restored synagogue and cultural landmarks, expressed her commitment to cultural revitalization. "Our cultural heritage is the soul of our community. By preserving and celebrating our traditions, we've not only rebuilt structures but also revived the spirit that defines us."

Rabbi Cohen, appreciating the efforts, said, "Cultural preservation is an ongoing journey. As we move forward, let's continue to weave our rich history into the fabric of our community."

President Martine, observing the Threads of Hope display, acknowledged the importance of community engagement. "Threads of Hope has become the tapestry that binds us together. Through open dialogue and understanding, we've sown the seeds of unity and collaboration."

Annette, who spearheaded Threads of Hope, added, "Our community members are the threads that weave the story of our collective journey. By actively engaging with their aspirations and concerns, we ensure that our city grows in harmony with the desires of its people."

Professor Sophie, amidst green spaces and eco-friendly buildings, spoke about the commitment to sustainability. "Our city has embraced a sustainable ethos. By integrating eco-friendly practices into our daily lives, we're sowing the seeds of environmental stewardship for the benefit of future generations."

Marcus, known for his sustainable investments, added, "Sustainability is not just a choice; it's a responsibility. Our commitment to green initiatives sets a standard for communities worldwide, showcasing that prosperity and environmental consciousness can coexist."

Jean-Claude, recognizing the potential of youth, discussed the initiatives for empowerment. "Our youth are the architects of the dynamic future we envision. By investing in their education, providing mentorship, and fostering a culture of innovation, we're sowing the seeds of a vibrant and resilient community."

President Martine, inspired by the vision, said, "The energy of our youth propels us forward. As we celebrate our achievements, let's ensure that we continue to provide them with the tools and opportunities they need to shape the destiny of our city."

The dialogue among the leaders encapsulated the essence of their collective vision. Annette, looking at the diverse group assembled, said, "Our journey is far from over, but today, as we stand on the foundation of our collective efforts, we can see the fruits of our labor."

President Martine, addressing the community, declared, "Our city, once scarred by adversity, has risen from the ashes. Today, we don't just rebuild; we sow the seeds of prosperity that will yield a harvest for generations to come."

The leaders, community members, and visionaries stood in unity, each face reflecting the pride and anticipation for the promising future they had collectively envisioned. As the sun climbed higher in the sky, casting a warm glow over the rejuvenated city, the dialogue concluded, and the leaders dispersed, each committed to nurturing the seeds of prosperity that would continue to flourish in the resilient soil of Port-au-Prince.

CHAPTER 36
TEMPLE OF TRANSFORMATION

The Temple of Transformation stood as a symbol of spiritual harmony and cultural unity within the heart of Port-au-Prince. Annette, Marcus, Professor Sophie, Jean-Claude, Sheikh Ahmed, Bishop Ruiz, Rabbi Cohen, and President Martine gathered within its sacred walls to discuss the next phase of their journey.

Annette, her eyes filled with reverence, spoke as they stood in the temple's serene courtyard. "In this sacred space, where faiths converge and spirits find solace, let us discuss the transformation our community seeks. The temple is a testament to the unity of our diverse beliefs, and within its embrace, we find strength to shape a future of profound transformation."

Sheikh Ahmed, representing the Islamic community, shared his thoughts. "The Temple of Transformation reflects the power of shared sacred spaces. Our commitment to unity and understanding fosters an environment where transformation becomes a collective journey."

Bishop Ruiz, his presence radiating warmth, added, "In the sanctuary of this temple, we recognize that transformation is not just individual; it's communal. Our shared faith in the potential of our community propels us forward."

Rabbi Cohen, standing beside the ark containing sacred scrolls, spoke, "The scrolls within this ark hold stories of resilience and hope.

As we contemplate transformation, let us draw inspiration from the narratives of our collective history."

Marcus, with a nod to the temple's architecture, remarked, "Economic transformation mirrors the grandeur of this temple. It requires a solid foundation, intricate planning, and a shared vision. Our investments have set the stage, but now we embark on a journey to sow seeds that will yield lasting prosperity."

Jean-Claude, the economist known for his innovative strategies, interjected, "Economic transformation is not just about financial gain; it's about uplifting lives. By fostering inclusive growth and sustainable practices, we ensure that our community thrives in harmony with its economic foundations."

Professor Sophie, her eyes lighting up with passion, addressed the role of education. "Just as the temple stands as a beacon of wisdom, education serves as the light guiding our community. By nurturing young minds and instilling a love for learning, we embark on a journey of transformative knowledge."

President Martine, embodying the spirit of leadership, asserted, "Transformation requires visionary leadership. Our community looks to each one of us to guide and inspire. Let us not only rebuild but lead by example, showing that through collaboration, we can achieve remarkable transformation."

Annette, reflecting on the Threads of Hope initiative, continued, "Threads of Hope weaves a tapestry of unity among our community members. As we discuss transformation, let us actively engage with the aspirations and dreams of our people, ensuring that the fabric of our shared future is strong and vibrant."

Rabbi Cohen, with a reverence for cultural heritage, expressed, "Cultural transformation is a celebration of diversity. As we breathe life into our traditions and honor our shared history, we create a community that embraces its cultural richness."

Professor Sophie, standing near the temple's lush gardens, emphasized sustainability. "The gardens surrounding this temple echo the harmony between nature and human endeavor. Our commitment to sustainable living ensures that our transformations leave a positive impact on the environment."

Sheikh Ahmed, appreciating the temple's inclusive atmosphere, stated, "In the realm of interfaith harmony, we witness the transformative power of unity. Let the Temple of Transformation be a reminder that our diverse beliefs can coexist, fostering a community that thrives on shared values."

Jean-Claude, recognizing the potential of the youth, declared, "The transformation of our community lies in the hands of our youth. Let us invest in their education, empower them with opportunities, and guide them to be catalysts for positive change."

As the dialogue unfolded within the sacred space, a collective vision emerged – a vision of holistic transformation that touched every facet of the community.

Annette, encapsulating the sentiments, said, "The Temple of Transformation is not merely a place of worship; it's a symbol of our shared commitment to evolve, uplift, and inspire. As we continue this journey, let our actions within these walls resonate with the transformative spirit we aim to cultivate."

President Martine, gazing at the temple's towering spires, concluded, "In the pursuit of transformation, let us be guided by the wisdom embedded in these stones.

May our community, like this temple, stand as a testament to the power of collective evolution, resilience, and shared aspirations."

The leaders exited the temple, carrying with them the essence of their dialogue – a commitment to transformative actions that would echo through the city, creating a legacy of enduring prosperity, unity, and spiritual harmony.

CHAPTER 37
HOPE IN THE HOTEL INDUSTRY

The sun dipped below the horizon, casting a warm glow over Port-au-Prince. Annette, Marcus, Professor Sophie, Jean-Claude, Sheikh Ahmed, Bishop Ruiz, Rabbi Cohen, and President Martine gathered in the lobby of a newly constructed hotel – a symbol of resilience and a beacon of hope for the city's future.

Annette, standing near the reception desk, addressed the group. "In the heart of our city, where once stood remnants of adversity, rises this hotel – a testament to our collective efforts. Today, we discuss not just the hospitality industry but the hope it brings for economic revival, cultural exchange, and a brighter future."

Marcus, known for his strategic investments, began with an economic insight. "The hotel industry is more than accommodation; it's an economic engine. Our investments have not only rebuilt structures but laid the foundation for a thriving hospitality sector that will contribute significantly to our city's economic resurgence."

Jean-Claude, the economist, added, "A flourishing hotel industry contributes not just to the economy but also to employment opportunities. It becomes a catalyst for growth, attracting tourists, events, and business activities that stimulate various sectors of our community."

Professor Sophie, considering the educational impact, spoke about the connection between the hotel industry and learning.

"Hotels offer a dynamic environment for experiential learning. From culinary arts to hospitality management, our youth can gain valuable skills and insights that extend beyond the confines of traditional classrooms."

Annette, passionate about cultural revitalization, shared her vision. "Hotels are more than structures; they are gateways to cultural exchange. By incorporating our local traditions, art, and cuisine, we not only attract visitors but also showcase the richness of our community's identity."

Sheikh Ahmed, appreciating the significance of hospitality, remarked, "In the Islamic tradition, hospitality is a revered virtue. Hotels, as spaces of welcome, embody the spirit of generosity and unity. They become bridges that connect diverse communities."

Bishop Ruiz, expressing his thoughts on the cultural significance, added, "Hotels, like our churches, synagogues, and mosques, become places of gathering. They hold the potential to host events that celebrate our shared humanity, fostering understanding and unity."

Rabbi Cohen, considering the interfaith aspect, said, "In the hotel industry, we have an opportunity to create spaces that embrace people from all walks of life. Whether for conferences, celebrations, or retreats, hotels can become hubs for interfaith dialogue and collaboration."

President Martine, embodying leadership, addressed the group. "As we discuss the role of hotels in our community, let us not forget their potential as symbols of our resilience. They stand as monuments to our ability to rise from adversity and offer a welcoming embrace to the world."

Marcus, with a focus on sustainability, spoke about the environmental responsibility of the hotel industry. "Sustainability is not just a trend; it's a necessity. Our hotels can lead the way in eco-friendly practices, showcasing that prosperity and environmental consciousness can coexist."

Annette, reflecting on community engagement, proposed, "Let our hotels be more than commercial spaces; let them be extensions of our community. Engaging local businesses, artists, and residents in hotel initiatives can create a symbiotic relationship that benefits everyone."

Professor Sophie, considering employment opportunities, emphasized, "Hotels, with their diverse departments, can become job hubs. From housekeeping to management, each role contributes to the hotel's success and provides valuable employment opportunities for our community members."

Jean-Claude, recognizing the potential for youth empowerment, declared, "Hotels can be platforms for our youth to showcase their talents. By integrating cultural performances, art exhibitions, and youth-driven initiatives, we ensure that our hotels become dynamic spaces for expression."

As the dialogue continued, a vision emerged – a collaborative effort to not only rebuild structures but to infuse the hotel industry with purpose, cultural richness, and a commitment to sustainable practices.

Amidst these discussions, a decision was made to open job applications for community members to work in the hotel. Thousands of job opportunities were created, providing employment for the people of Port-au-Prince.

Annette, joyfully announcing the initiative, said, "Our community deserves to benefit directly from this venture. By opening job opportunities, we not only provide employment but also foster a sense of ownership and pride in our shared success."

President Martine, pleased with the outcome, added, "This is not just a hotel; it's an economic catalyst for our community. With jobs created, revenue generated, and a commitment to sustainability, we are shaping a future where Port-au-Prince thrives."

As the news of job openings spread, the community embraced the opportunity, and applications flooded in. The hotel lobby, once a symbolic gathering place for leaders, transformed into a bustling hub of activity as hopeful individuals sought employment.

In the lobby's midst, Annette, smiling at the sight of eager applicants, remarked, "Our hotels are not just accommodations; they are ambassadors of our community. Let us embark on a journey where the hospitality industry becomes a driving force for economic growth, cultural preservation, and a source of pride for every resident of Port-au-Prince."

President Martine, looking around the bustling lobby, concluded, "In the lobby of this hotel, we don't just see furniture and décor; we see the stories of our journey. Each guest who walks through these doors becomes a part of our narrative. May our hotels be beacons of hospitality, warmth, and hope – inviting the world to experience the spirit of Port-au-Prince." As the leaders dispersed, the hotel's doors remained open, welcoming a future where the industry would not only provide accommodation but also serve as a catalyst for the city's prosperity, cultural exchange, and a testament to the resilient spirit that defined Port-au-Prince.

CHAPTER 38
ANNETTE'S WAR ON POVERTY

The morning sunbathed Port-au-Prince in golden hues as Annette convened a gathering of leaders in a community center nestled amidst the vibrant city. Marcus, Professor Sophie, Jean-Claude, Sheikh Ahmed, Bishop Ruiz, Rabbi Cohen, and President Martine gathered, their presence resonating with purpose.

Annette, with unwavering determination, addressed the group. "Today, we embark on a new front in our mission. Poverty is a formidable adversary, but together, we shall wage a war on its roots. Let our efforts be a beacon of hope, illuminating a path towards economic empowerment, education, and a brighter future for every citizen of Port-au-Prince."

Marcus spoke first. "To win this war, we must empower our community economically. Initiatives like microfinance, local business support, and job creation can be our arsenal. By fostering economic resilience, we not only alleviate poverty but also fortify the foundations of our society."

Professor Sophie, an advocate for education, added, "Education is our greatest weapon. Let us invest in schools, scholarships, and vocational training programs. By empowering minds, we break the chains of poverty and nurture a generation capable of transforming their destinies."

Jean-Claude, the seasoned economist, shared his insights. "Economic policies must be inclusive. By creating an environment that encourages entrepreneurship, innovation, and sustainable growth, we set the stage for a community that thrives collectively, leaving no one behind in the war against poverty."

Sheikh Ahmed, representing the Islamic community, emphasized community support. "In the spirit of solidarity, let us establish support networks. Initiatives like community kitchens, health clinics, and collaborative efforts will ensure that the burden of poverty is eased collectively."

Bishop Ruiz, with a focus on spiritual well-being, added, "Poverty is not just a material challenge; it tests the spirit. Let our churches, mosques, and synagogues become beacons of hope and resilience. Through spiritual guidance, we can uplift those facing the harshest realities."

Rabbi Cohen, championing cultural richness, spoke next. "Poverty often erodes cultural identity. Let us ensure that our cultural heritage is preserved through art, festivals, and initiatives that celebrate diversity. This cultural wealth will become a source of strength in our war against poverty."

President Martine, the embodiment of leadership, rallied the group. "Our strategies are powerful, but they require collective action. As we wage this war, let us remember that our greatest victories will be measured by the lives we uplift, the children we educate, and the families we empower. This is a battle we must win for the soul of our community."

Annette, envisioning community engagement, concluded, "Our success depends on the active involvement of every citizen.

Threads of Hope will extend beyond dialogue; it will weave into the fabric of our community, binding us together in the shared commitment to eradicate poverty and build a future where every individual thrives."

The leaders engaged in a spirited dialogue, exchanging ideas, concerns, and visions. They discussed the specifics of their strategies, debated the nuances of implementation, and shared stories of individuals impacted by poverty. The exchange of perspectives enriched their collective understanding and fueled their determination.

In the culmination of their dialogue, the leaders stood united, hands joined, pledging to wage this war on poverty with unwavering commitment. Annette's words echoed in the air, "Let our unity be the force that drives out poverty, opening avenues of prosperity and hope for our community."

As they dispersed, the leaders carried with them a shared vision and a commitment to turn the tide against poverty. The war they declared was not just a battle of policies and programs; it was a collective endeavor to uplift the human spirit, empower lives, and script a narrative of triumph over adversity in the resilient heart of Port-au-Prince.

CHAPTER 39
JEAN-CLAUDE'S REVOLUTION

The streets of Port-au-Prince pulsed with life as Jean-Claude, a charismatic and impassioned leader, addressed a diverse crowd gathered in a makeshift square. Annette, Marcus, Professor Sophie, Jean-Claude, Sheikh Ahmed, Bishop Ruiz, Rabbi Cohen, and President Martine stood among the eager faces, sensing the charged atmosphere of change.

Jean-Claude Desmarais, with his years of experience as an economist and his deep commitment to community prosperity, took center stage amidst the gathered crowd. His voice resonated with a calm authority as he began to address the eager faces before him.

"My fellow citizens," Jean-Claude started, his tone measured yet impassioned, "I stand before you today not only as an economist but as a member of this community, driven by the same desire for positive change that has brought us all together here."

Jean-Claude, his voice carrying the weight of conviction, spoke, "Today marks the beginning of a revolution, not of violence, but of transformation. A revolution that will reshape the very fabric of our community, dismantling the barriers of poverty, injustice, and inequality."

A murmur of agreement rippled through the crowd, with nods of approval and anticipation.

Jean-Claude continued, "Jean-Claude's revolution is indeed a call for transformation, and I believe that economic empowerment lies at the heart of this endeavor. We must dismantle the barriers that hinder our community's economic progress and build a foundation of prosperity that benefits each and every one of us."

A hand shot up from the crowd, and Jean-Claude nodded in acknowledgment, inviting the question.

"How do you intend to tackle the economic challenges that our community faces?" a voice from the crowd inquired.

Jean-Claude's gaze swept across the audience before settling on the speaker. "It's an excellent question," he replied, his voice carrying a note of enthusiasm. "First and foremost, we must ensure that our economic strategies prioritize inclusivity. This means implementing microfinance initiatives that provide access to capital for aspiring entrepreneurs, supporting local businesses through targeted assistance programs, and promoting sustainable economic practices that benefit both our community and the environment."

Another voice chimed in from the crowd, "But what about job opportunities? How do we ensure that everyone has access to meaningful employment?"

Jean-Claude nodded thoughtfully, acknowledging the validity of the concern. "Creating job opportunities is indeed crucial," he affirmed. "That's why we need to focus on sectors that have the potential for growth and development, such as renewable energy, agriculture, and information technology. By investing in these areas and providing the necessary training and support, we can ensure that our community members have the skills and opportunities they need to thrive in the modern economy."

A sense of optimism began to permeate the crowd as Jean-Claude outlined his vision for economic empowerment. Hands shot up one after another, eager to engage in the dialogue and contribute their own ideas and questions.

"How do we ensure that our economic initiatives are sustainable in the long term?" a voice from the back of the crowd asked.

Jean-Claude smiled, appreciating the thoughtful inquiry. "Sustainability is indeed a key consideration," he responded. "That's why we need to integrate environmental considerations into our economic planning and development. By prioritizing sustainable practices such as renewable energy, waste reduction, and eco-friendly infrastructure, we can ensure that our economic growth is not only beneficial but also sustainable for future generations."

The dialogue between Jean-Claude and the community members continued, each question and answer adding another layer of depth to the discussion. It was clear that Jean-Claude's vision for economic empowerment resonated deeply with the crowd, inspiring hope and determination for a brighter future for all.

Annette, standing beside Jean-Claude, added her support. "This is a revolution rooted in hope, unity, and the unwavering belief that every citizen has the right to a future defined by dignity and opportunity. Together, we shall embark on this transformative journey."

Marcus addressed the economic aspect. "Jean-Claude's revolution starts with economic empowerment. Our community needs access to resources, job opportunities, and fair economic policies. Let us dismantle the structures that perpetuate inequality and build a foundation of prosperity for all."

Professor Sophie, championing education, continued, "The revolution must reach our classrooms. We need educational reform that ensures every child, regardless of background, receives quality education. Knowledge is the greatest catalyst for change, and we must empower our youth with it."

Jean-Claude, the seasoned economist, added his insights. "Our economic strategies must prioritize inclusivity. Microfinance initiatives, support for local businesses, and sustainable economic practices will create a level playing field, ensuring that every citizen can contribute to and benefit from our community's growth."

Sheikh Ahmed, representing the Islamic community, spoke of unity. "Jean-Claude's revolution is not limited by faith or background. It is a call for unity among us all. In the spirit of interfaith collaboration, let us forge a path where diversity is our strength, not a source of division."

Bishop Ruiz, focusing on social justice, declared, "The revolution must address the inequities that plague our society. Let us stand against discrimination, advocate for the marginalized, and create a community where every individual is treated with fairness and compassion."

Rabbi Cohen, emphasizing cultural harmony, added, "Our cultural richness is a source of strength. Jean-Claude's revolution should celebrate and preserve our diverse heritage, fostering an environment where every individual feels a sense of belonging."

President Martine, embodying leadership, called the community to action. "This revolution demands active participation from each of us. Whether through community initiatives, volunteering, or simply treating our neighbors with respect, let us all contribute to the transformation we aspire to achieve."

The leaders engaged in a dialogue with the community, listening to their concerns, hopes, and aspirations. The exchange of ideas created a tapestry of perspectives that would guide the revolution. Jean-Claude encouraged open dialogue, stating, "Our strength lies in our ability to listen, understand, and work together. This revolution is not mine alone; it belongs to each of you."

Annette, inspired by the Threads of Hope initiative, proposed its extension. "Let Threads of Hope weave through Jean-Claude's revolution. It's not just a symbol; it's a tangible expression of our unity. Through Threads of Hope, we can connect hearts, share stories, and build bridges that transcend differences."

As the dialogue unfolded, the leaders and the community members formed a symbolic circle, pledging unity in the pursuit of Jean-Claude's revolution. Hand in hand, they vowed to be architects of a future where every individual had the opportunity to thrive, unburdened by the chains of inequality.

Jean-Claude, concluding the gathering, addressed the crowd with fervor. "This revolution is not a fleeting moment; it is a movement that will shape the destiny of Port-au-Prince. Together, with courage, compassion, and a collective commitment to change, we will herald an era where justice, equality, and prosperity prevail."

As the sun dipped below the horizon, casting a warm glow on the gathering, the revolutionary spirit echoed through the streets of Port-au-Prince. Jean-Claude's vision had ignited a flame of hope that would burn bright, guiding the community toward a future where the echoes of change transformed the very soul of the city.

CHAPTER 40
SCHOOLING THE STREETS

Annette stood alongside Marcus, Professor Sophie, Jean-Claude, Sheikh Ahmed, Bishop Ruiz, Rabbi Cohen, and President Martine in a lively neighborhood in Port-au-Prince. They were at the entrance of a vibrant community school that aimed to bring education to the streets, breaking down barriers and fostering a love for learning.

Annette, with a gleam of excitement in her eyes, addressed the group gathered in the vibrant streets of Port-au-Prince.

"Welcome to a revolutionary concept – Schooling the Streets," she exclaimed, her voice filled with passion. "Our mission is to take education beyond traditional classrooms and bring it to the very heart of our community. This is not just a school; it's a transformative space where every street becomes a pathway to knowledge."

She paused, allowing her words to sink in before continuing.

"Imagine children learning not only from textbooks but from the world around them – from the bustling markets, the colorful murals adorning our streets, and the stories of our community members," Annette enthused. "Schooling the Streets will blur the lines between formal education and real-life experiences, making learning truly immersive and engaging."

Annette outlined her vision for Schooling the Streets, emphasizing its role in addressing the unique challenges faced by Haiti's education system.

"We will empower our community members to become educators," she declared. "Through training programs and workshops, we will equip parents, elders, and local artisans with the tools to share their knowledge and skills with the next generation."

She continued, "We will leverage technology to reach even the most remote areas, providing access to quality educational resources through mobile learning platforms and interactive digital tools."

Annette's vision extended beyond academic learning to encompass holistic development.

"We will prioritize the well-being of our students," she asserted. "Schooling the Streets will not only nurture their intellectual growth but also support their physical, emotional, and social development. We will create safe spaces where children can express themselves freely, fostering creativity and self-confidence."

As Annette spoke, she invited questions from the community members, eager to address any concerns or doubts they might have.

A community member raised their hand, voicing a common concern. "How will you ensure that children receive a well-rounded education without traditional classrooms?"

Annette smiled warmly, ready to provide an answer. "Our curriculum will be multidisciplinary, incorporating elements of literacy, numeracy, science, art, and practical life skills," she explained. "We will integrate project-based learning, allowing students to explore topics that interest them and apply their knowledge in real-world contexts."

Another community member expressed skepticism about the feasibility of the initiative. "How will you fund Schooling the Streets, and what about resources like books and materials?"

Annette nodded, acknowledging the valid concern. "We will seek support from local businesses, community organizations, and international partners," she replied. "Additionally, we will utilize recycled materials and digital resources to minimize costs. Our focus will be on creativity and innovation, making the most of the resources available to us."

As the dialogue continued, Annette addressed each question and concern with confidence and clarity, drawing upon her passion for education and her unwavering belief in the transformative power of Schooling the Streets.

In conclusion, she reiterated her commitment to the vision, inspired by the potential to revolutionize education in Haiti.

"Schooling the Streets is not just a dream – it's a tangible opportunity to redefine education for our country," Annette declared, her voice ringing with conviction. "Together, we can create a learning environment that empowers our children, strengthens our communities, and paves the way for a brighter future for Haiti."

After outlining her vision for Schooling the Streets, Annette turned to the rest of the leaders, her eyes shining with anticipation.

"Does anyone have anything to add or any thoughts they'd like to share?" she inquired, inviting their input.

President Martine, with a nod of approval, stepped forward, her expression reflecting a sense of solidarity with Annette's vision.

"Annette's proposal is not only innovative but also aligns with our government's commitment to transforming our education system," she affirmed. "Schooling the Streets has the potential to revolutionize learning in Haiti and empower our youth to reach their full potential."

Professor Sophie, known for her dedication to educational reform, spoke next. "I wholeheartedly support Annette's initiative," she stated. "As educators, it's our responsibility to meet students where they are and provide them with opportunities to thrive. Schooling the Streets offers a holistic approach to education that fosters creativity, critical thinking, and lifelong learning."

Jean-Claude, the economist, chimed in, emphasizing the economic benefits of investing in education. "Education is not just a social good; it's also an economic imperative," he asserted. "By equipping our youth with the skills and knowledge they need to succeed, we are investing in Haiti's future workforce and driving sustainable economic growth."

Sheikh Ahmed, appreciating the initiative's focus on community engagement, shared his perspective. "Education is a shared responsibility that extends beyond the classroom," he remarked. "By involving parents, elders, and community members in the learning process, we create a sense of ownership and collective responsibility for our children's education."

Bishop Ruiz, known for his commitment to social justice, offered words of encouragement. "Education is a powerful tool for social change," he affirmed. "Schooling the Streets has the potential to break down barriers and empower marginalized communities, paving the way for a more equitable and inclusive society."

Rabbi Cohen, with a nod of agreement, expressed his support for the initiative's emphasis on cultural preservation. "Our cultural heritage is an integral part of who we are," he stated. "By incorporating local traditions, art, and history into the curriculum, Schooling the Streets celebrates our diversity and fosters a sense of pride in our identity."

Annette listened intently to their feedback, feeling inspired by their support and encouraged by their shared commitment to transforming education in Haiti.

As the dialogue concluded, Annette drew her conclusions, her voice filled with determination. "Thank you all for your valuable input and support," she said, addressing the group. "With our collective efforts and unwavering dedication, I believe that Schooling the Streets has the potential to revolutionize education in Haiti and create a brighter future for our children."

The leaders nodded in agreement, united in their shared vision for a more inclusive, equitable, and transformative education system in Haiti.

The leaders engaged in a dialogue with community members, parents, and students who were eager to share their thoughts on Schooling the Streets. The exchange of ideas enriched the vision, and the leaders listened attentively to the aspirations and concerns voiced by those directly impacted.

Annette, inspired by the Threads of Hope initiative, proposed its integration into Schooling the Streets. "Threads of Hope will connect the stories of our community. Through art, literature, and storytelling, we can weave a tapestry that reflects the unique narratives of every student and celebrates the triumphs of learning in unexpected places."

The inauguration of Schooling the Streets was marked by a vibrant ceremony. Children, clad in school uniforms, lined up eagerly as Annette cut the ribbon, symbolizing the opening of this unconventional space for learning. Laughter, excitement, and a sense of possibility filled the air.

President Martine, addressing the gathered crowd, declared, "Today, we witness the birth of a new era in education. Schooling the Streets is not just a school; it's a manifestation of our commitment to the potential that resides within every child. This initiative embodies the resilience and innovative spirit of our community."

Annette, surrounded by the energy of the moment, shared her words of hope. "Schooling the Streets is a symbol of our belief that education is a right, not a privilege. Let this be a space where dreams are nurtured, potential is unlocked, and every child finds the key to a future filled with possibilities."

In the days following the inauguration, Schooling the Streets became a hub of community engagement. Workshops, cultural events, and collaborative projects encouraged active participation from parents, residents, and local businesses, turning the school into a vibrant center of learning and communal growth.

The leaders observed firsthand the impact of Schooling the Streets on students. Engaged, enthusiastic, and filled with a renewed sense of curiosity, the children embraced learning in this unconventional setting. They shared stories, explored new ideas, and reveled in the joy of discovering knowledge right on the streets they called home.

As the day came to a close, Annette stood at the entrance of Schooling the Streets, reflecting on the transformative power of education. "Today, we have not just opened a school; we have opened doors of opportunity, curiosity, and hope. Schooling the Streets is a testament to the belief that education can flourish in the most unexpected places, lighting up the future of our community one lesson at a time."

The leaders left the vibrant atmosphere of Schooling the Streets, knowing that they had sown the seeds for a future where education would not be confined by walls but would thrive on the streets, reaching every corner of the community and cultivating a generation of empowered, inspired learners.

CHAPTER 41
BISHOP RUIZ'S SERMON OF UNITY

An announcement echoed through the community, calling everyone to gather at a designated spot, eager to hear Bishop Ruiz deliver a message on Unity. The anticipation electrified the air as the whole community responded with enthusiasm and positivity.

Bishop Ruiz, a figure of wisdom and compassion, prepared to deliver a sermon that transcended religious boundaries. Annette, Marcus, Professor Sophie, Jean-Claude, Sheikh Ahmed, Rabbi Cohen, and President Martine stood among the congregation, embodying the diverse unity that defined their community.

Bishop Ruiz, standing tall at the makeshift podium, began with a solemn blessing. "Dear friends," he began, his voice carrying across the gathered crowd, "today we come together not as members of different faiths but as one community, bound by the threads of shared humanity. Let this moment be a testament to the unity that defines us."

He paused, allowing his words to sink in before continuing.

"Unity is not merely the absence of conflict but the presence of understanding, empathy, and mutual respect," Bishop Ruiz elaborated, his gaze sweeping across the attentive faces before him. "It is the recognition of our interconnectedness and the celebration of our diversity. In times of hardship and adversity, it is our unity that sustains us, giving us the strength to overcome challenges together."

Bishop Ruiz invited questions from the community members, encouraging an open dialogue.

A community member raised their hand, voicing a common concern. "How can we foster unity in our community amidst differences in beliefs and backgrounds?"

Bishop Ruiz nodded, acknowledging the importance of the question. "Unity begins with dialogue and a willingness to listen to one another," he responded. "It requires us to look beyond our differences and find common ground based on our shared values and aspirations. Through respectful communication and collaboration, we can build bridges that unite us rather than divide us."

Another community member expressed skepticism about the feasibility of achieving unity. "Is unity truly attainable, or is it merely an idealistic notion?"

Bishop Ruiz smiled warmly, ready to address the doubt. "While achieving unity may not always be easy, it is certainly attainable," he affirmed. "It requires effort, patience, and a commitment to finding common ground. By focusing on our shared humanity and working together towards common goals, we can create a community where unity flourishes."

After addressing the questions from the community members, Bishop Ruiz turned to the rest of the leaders gathered with a gracious nod. "Do any of my esteemed colleagues have anything to add to our discussion on unity?" he inquired, inviting their input.

President Martine stepped forward, her expression reflecting a sense of solidarity with Bishop Ruiz's message. "Bishop Ruiz has eloquently captured the essence of unity," she stated.

"As leaders, it is our responsibility to lead by example and foster an environment where unity thrives. Together, we can inspire our community to embrace diversity and work towards a common vision of harmony and peace."

Professor Sophie, known for her dedication to social justice, spoke next. "Unity is not just a lofty ideal but a practical necessity," she asserted. "In a world fraught with division and discord, it is through unity that we find strength and resilience. Let us strive to cultivate unity in our community, celebrating our differences and finding strength in our shared humanity."

As the dialogue continued, Bishop Ruiz listened intently to the perspectives shared by the other leaders, feeling inspired by their commitment to fostering unity in the community. Together, they stood united in their shared vision of building a community where understanding, empathy, and mutual respect flourished, paving the way for a brighter future for all.

Annette, stepping forward, added, "Bishop Ruiz's sermon is a celebration of our diversity and a reminder that, despite our differences, we share a common purpose – to build a community that stands strong in unity."

Bishop Ruiz, his voice resonating with warmth, addressed the crowd. "In our diversity lies our strength. Each one of us is a unique thread in the rich tapestry of our community. Today, I invite you to embrace the beauty of our differences, for it is in unity that we find our true strength."

Sheikh Ahmed, standing beside Bishop Ruiz, added, "Unity is not the absence of differences but the ability to coexist with them. Our faiths may differ, but our humanity unites us. Let us celebrate the mosaic of beliefs that enrich our community."

Rabbi Cohen, representing the Jewish community, shared, "Our various faiths may have different rituals, traditions, and scriptures, but at the core, we share fundamental values – compassion, justice, and love. Let these shared values be the foundation of our unity."

Marcus, known for his economic insights, related unity to prosperity. "Economic unity is vital. When we support local businesses, invest in sustainable practices, and create opportunities for all, we not only strengthen our economy but also foster a sense of collective prosperity that benefits everyone."

The leaders engaged in a dialogue with community members, listening to their thoughts on unity. They discussed the challenges faced by the community, the power of collaboration, and the importance of fostering an environment where everyone felt heard and valued.

To symbolize unity, Bishop Ruiz invited representatives from different faiths, community groups, and leaders to join hands in a symbolic circle. The act represented the interconnectedness of the community and the strength that came from standing together.

Bishop Ruiz, leading a prayer, said, "In this moment of unity, let our hearts beat as one. May we find strength in our diversity, compassion in our differences, and love that transcends all boundaries. Bless our community with the power of unity."

As the sermon concluded, Annette stepped forward once more. "Bishop Ruiz's words resonate deeply within us. Let this sermon be a reminder that, despite the challenges we face, our unity is an unbreakable bond that will guide us towards a future where compassion, understanding, and shared purpose prevail."

In the aftermath of the sermon, community members shared their reflections. The atmosphere was one of unity, understanding, and a renewed commitment to fostering a community where diversity was not a source of division but a wellspring of strength.

President Martine, looking at the united community, shared her vision. "This sermon of unity is not just a one-time event; it's a guiding principle for our future. Let us carry the spirit of unity in our hearts, weaving it into the very fabric of our community's identity."

As the congregation dispersed, the essence of Bishop Ruiz's sermon lingered in the air – a gentle reminder that, in unity, the community found its greatest strength, transcending differences to forge a shared destiny grounded in compassion, respect, and the beauty of diversity.

CHAPTER 42
HAITI'S SYMPHONY

After a beautiful sermon on Unity delivered by Bishop Ruiz, the city resonated with the vibrant spirit of unity in the heart of Port-au-Prince. Annette, Marcus, Professor Sophie, Jean-Claude, Sheikh Ahmed, Bishop Ruiz, Rabbi Cohen, and President Martine gathered in a community center for an event that would symbolize the harmonious blend of Haiti's diverse threads.

Annette stood at the podium, her eyes reflecting the energy of the moment. "Welcome, dear friends, to Haiti's Symphony – an ode to our diverse community, where each individual is a unique note contributing to a melody that defines us. Today, we celebrate the beauty of our differences, weaving them into a harmonious tapestry that resonates with the essence of Haiti."

Marcus addressed the economic aspect. "Just as in a symphony every instrument plays a crucial role, our economy thrives when we embrace diversity. Supporting local businesses, investing in sustainable practices, and creating economic opportunities for all contribute to the economic harmony of our community."

Professor Sophie added, "Our schools should be dynamic centers of learning, nurturing the individual strengths and talents of each student. By fostering an environment that embraces diverse learning styles and backgrounds, we create a symphony of knowledge that enriches us all."

Jean-Claude contributed his perspective. "Economic harmony is achieved through inclusive economic strategies. Microfinance initiatives, vocational training programs, and support for small businesses compose the notes of a resilient and thriving economic symphony."

Sheikh Ahmed, representing the Islamic community, spoke of interfaith collaboration. "Just as diverse musical instruments come together to create a symphony, our faiths harmonize when we collaborate. Interfaith dialogue and understanding form the foundation of a spiritual symphony that echoes throughout our community."

Bishop Ruiz, focusing on social harmony, declared, "Our social fabric is a symphony of stories, experiences, and perspectives. When we prioritize social justice, inclusivity, and compassion, we compose a harmonious society where every individual contributes to the collective well-being."

Rabbi Cohen, appreciating cultural richness, added, "Cultural diversity is the melody of our community. Each cultural note contributes to the vibrant composition of Haiti's Symphony. Let us celebrate and preserve our unique traditions, for they are the soulful threads that weave our collective identity."

President Martine, embodying leadership, addressed the crowd. "As leaders, our role is to conduct this symphony with wisdom and fairness. Through policies that promote equality, justice, and unity, we ensure that every member of our community has a voice in the beautiful symphony we collectively create."

Annette, inspired by the Threads of Hope initiative, proposed its integration into Haiti's Symphony. "Threads of Hope will be the visual representation of our diverse notes coming together.

Each thread, unique in color and texture, contributes to the overall richness of our community's symphony. Let us weave a tapestry that tells the story of Haiti's unity in diversity."

The event featured musical performances that showcased the diversity of Haiti's musical heritage. From traditional folk tunes to modern compositions, each piece echoed the cultural richness of the community. The musicians, representing various backgrounds, played in harmony, symbolizing the unity that can be achieved through the celebration of differences.

Following the performances, community members engaged in a dialogue about the significance of Haiti's Symphony. They shared personal stories, discussed the impact of diversity on their lives, and explored ways to strengthen the harmonious bonds that connected them all.

In a symbolic gesture, community leaders and members formed a circle, pledging unity and harmony. Hand in hand, they vowed to uphold the principles of equality, respect, and collaboration that would allow Haiti's Symphony to resonate throughout the generations.

As the event drew to a close, Annette took the stage once more. "Haiti's Symphony is not a one-time celebration; it is a living composition that continues to evolve with each passing day. Let our commitment to unity and diversity be the guiding notes in the ongoing symphony of our community."

President Martine, looking towards the future, shared her vision. "May Haiti's Symphony be a legacy that transcends time, echoing the resilience, strength, and beauty of our community. Through every challenge and triumph, may our diverse notes continue to blend into a melody that defines the soul of Port-au-Prince."

As the community dispersed, the echoes of Haiti's Symphony lingered in the air—a powerful reminder that, in unity and diversity, the people of Haiti had created a symphony that celebrated their shared humanity and embraced the richness of their collective identity.

CHAPTER 43
A NEW DAWN FOR HAITI

The dawn of a new day bathed the streets of Port-au-Prince in a warm, golden glow. Annette, Marcus, Professor Sophie, Jean-Claude, Sheikh Ahmed, Bishop Ruiz, Rabbi Cohen, and President Martine gathered at a symbolic location – a plaza that had once been a focal point of struggle and despair. Today, it would witness a transformative event, marking the beginning of a hopeful chapter in Haiti's history.

Annette stood before the crowd; her gaze filled with determination. "Today, we stand on sacred ground, a place that has witnessed the resilience of our people in the face of adversity. We gather not to dwell on the past, but to usher in a new dawn for Haiti, a dawn that eclipses despair and ushers in hope."

Marcus, addressing the economic aspect, shared his vision. "Economic renewal is the key to Haiti's resurgence. By investing in sustainable projects, supporting local businesses, and creating job opportunities, we pave the way for a brighter future where economic stability is a reality for all."

Professor Sophie, championing education, added, "The path to a new dawn requires an empowered and educated youth. Let us revitalize our education system, providing quality learning opportunities for every child. Education is the beacon that guides a nation toward progress."

Jean-Claude, the seasoned economist, contributed his insights. "Our economic strategies must be forward-thinking. By fostering innovation, embracing sustainable practices, and attracting global investments, we position Haiti as a hub for growth and development."

Sheikh Ahmed, emphasizing unity, spoke of its role in rebuilding. "Unity is our strength. As we rebuild, let us celebrate our diversity, recognizing that it is our collective strength. Together, we can overcome any challenge and build a nation where every voice is heard."

Bishop Ruiz, focusing on the emotional healing of the nation, declared, "For a new dawn to truly emerge, we must heal the wounds of the past. Let forgiveness be the foundation upon which we rebuild our community, understanding that only through unity can we overcome the scars of despair."

Rabbi Cohen, appreciating cultural richness, added, "Our culture is a source of resilience. As we embark on this journey, let us preserve and celebrate our heritage. Cultural resilience will be the anchor that grounds us in the face of challenges."

President Martine, embodying leadership, addressed the crowd. "The responsibility of leadership is to guide a nation toward a brighter future. Let our actions be a testament to our commitment to a new Haiti, where every citizen can aspire to a life of dignity, opportunity, and fulfillment."

Annette added "Threads of Hope will weave through our rebuilding efforts, connecting hearts and stories. Each thread represents a commitment to a shared future, where despair is eclipsed by the collective hope of our people."

To symbolize growth and renewal, the leaders and community members participated in a symbolic tree planting ceremony. As the first roots touched the soil, the message was clear – a new Haiti was taking root, grounded in resilience, unity, and the promise of a better tomorrow.

The event transitioned into a community dialogue, where leaders and citizens engaged in open discussions about the collective vision for Haiti's future. They envisioned vibrant neighborhoods, thriving businesses, empowered individuals, and a nation that stood as a beacon of resilience and hope.

The plaza came alive with artistic expressions of hope – murals, sculptures, and performances that captured the spirit of Haiti's renewal. Local artists, inspired by the theme of a new dawn, contributed to the visual tapestry that would define this chapter in the nation's history.

As the day unfolded, Annette stood once more at the center of the plaza. "Today marks the beginning of a journey – a journey toward a new dawn for Haiti. Let our collective efforts, dreams, and determination be the driving force that propels our nation forward."

President Martine, looking toward the horizon, added, "I stand before you with a commitment to lead Haiti into a future defined by resilience, unity, and prosperity. Together, we will rise from the ashes of despair, embracing the dawn of a new era."

The day concluded with a closing ceremony, where the community members released lanterns into the night sky. Each lantern carried with it the aspirations, dreams, and hopes of a community determined to forge a path toward a brighter future.

As the lanterns ascended, their glow illuminated the faces of the gathered crowd, symbolizing the collective spirit that would guide Haiti through the challenges ahead. Eclipsing despair, the people of Haiti stepped into the embrace of a new dawn, united in their vision for a resilient, empowered, and hopeful nation.

CHAPTER 44
BREAKING CHAINS

The international leaders gathered once more, their collective resolve echoing in the halls of diplomacy. Annette, Marcus, Professor Sophie, Jean-Claude, Sheikh Ahmed, Bishop Ruiz, Rabbi Cohen, and President Martine knew that the journey toward a new dawn for Haiti would require confronting one of the darkest shadows that loomed over the nation – the control of gangs that had held the country captive for far too long.

In a secure meeting room, adorned with symbols of hope and resilience, the leaders discussed the pressing issue at hand. President Martine, with a sense of urgency, addressed the group, "We cannot build a new Haiti while shackled by the chains of criminal gangs. It's time to confront this challenge head-on, for the sake of our people and the vision we collectively share."

The room hummed with tension as intelligence reports were presented, detailing the networks, leaders, and operations of the gangs that had plagued Haiti. Annette, her eyes unwavering, acknowledged the severity of the situation. "These criminal networks are entrenched, but we cannot allow them to continue dictating the narrative of our nation."

Sheikh Ahmed emphasized the importance of global cooperation, stating, "This is not just Haiti's struggle; it is a challenge that requires international collaboration.

We must work together, pooling resources, intelligence, and strategies to dismantle these criminal networks and free the people of Haiti from their grip."

Marcus, bringing his economic insights to the table, suggested an economic strategy. "Eradicating the influence of these gangs requires addressing the root causes – poverty, lack of opportunities, and social inequality. Let us invest in economic development projects that create jobs, empower communities, and break the cycle of violence."

Bishop Ruiz, focusing on the human aspect, urged for a holistic approach. "As we dismantle these criminal networks, we must also provide avenues for healing and rehabilitation. Many of these individuals are products of a system that failed them. Let us not only break chains but mend broken spirits."

Rabbi Cohen, invoking the power of interfaith unity, proposed outreach programs. "Our faith communities can play a crucial role in bridging gaps and fostering understanding. Let us engage with religious leaders within the affected communities, offering support and guidance towards a path of peace."

President Martine, the beacon of leadership, issued a directive. "It's time for decisive action. Our international coalition will support Haitian law enforcement, strengthen border controls, and provide resources for community programs. We will not rest until the people of Haiti are free from the grip of these criminal networks."

The leaders agreed on a coordinated approach, involving intelligence agencies, law enforcement, and community engagement.

Their plan encompassed targeted operations to dismantle the top echelons of the criminal networks while simultaneously implementing programs to address the underlying socio-economic issues.

Annette emphasized the importance of engaging with local leaders who understood the intricacies of the communities affected. "We need the support of those who have the trust of the people. By collaborating with community leaders, we can ensure that our actions are rooted in the realities of the streets."

Sheikh Ahmed, speaking directly to the international community, appealed for support. "Haiti stands at a critical juncture. The success of our mission depends on the collective commitment of the global community. Let us stand together in solidarity, sending a clear message that criminality will not prevail."

Marcus proposed economic incentives for communities that actively participated in eradicating gang influence. "By providing economic opportunities and rewards for communities that actively contribute to the dismantling of these networks, we create a system where the people themselves become champions of change."

As the meeting concluded, Annette addressed the group, "We face a formidable adversary, but the strength of our collective will surpass any challenge. Together, we will break the chains that have bound Haiti for too long and pave the way for a new era of freedom, prosperity, and hope."

The international leaders, armed with a comprehensive strategy and a shared determination, embarked on the journey to liberate Haiti from the shadows of criminal control.

Coordinated operations, community engagement, economic initiatives, and global collaboration marked the beginning of a focused effort to break the chains that had hindered Haiti's progress for years.

In the streets of Port-au-Prince, where shadows had lingered for too long, the people began to sense a shift. The international leaders, standing united with the people of Haiti, were determined to confront the shadows and lead the nation toward the promise of a new dawn.

CHAPTER 45
EMBRACING PEACE

The outcome of the international leaders' decision to confront the criminal gangs in Haiti was nothing short of transformative. As their coordinated efforts unfolded, peace began to replace the shadows of fear and violence that had plagued the nation for far too long.

Annette, Marcus, Professor Sophie, Jean-Claude, Sheikh Ahmed, Bishop Ruiz, Rabbi Cohen, and President Martine witnessed firsthand the positive impact of their decisive action. Through targeted operations, community engagement, and economic initiatives, the grip of criminal networks gradually loosened, paving the way for a new era of calm and stability.

In the aftermath of the international coalition's intervention, the streets of Port-au-Prince underwent a profound transformation. Where once there were echoes of gunshots and the whispers of fear, there was now a sense of serenity and hope. Communities that had long been held hostage by violence began to reclaim their neighborhoods, rebuilding trust and fostering a spirit of cooperation.

Economic initiatives spearheaded by Marcus and Jean-Claude provided opportunities for employment and entrepreneurship, empowering individuals to break free from the cycle of poverty and violence. Microfinance programs, vocational training, and support for local businesses breathed new life into the economy, creating a ripple effect of prosperity that reached every corner of the community.

The holistic approach advocated by Bishop Ruiz and Rabbi Cohen ensured that the healing process extended beyond physical reconstruction. Rehabilitation programs offered a path to redemption for former gang members, addressing the root causes of violence and providing avenues for reconciliation and forgiveness.

Through interfaith outreach programs championed by Sheikh Ahmed and Rabbi Cohen, bridges of understanding were built among diverse communities. Faith leaders played a pivotal role in promoting dialogue and fostering a culture of peace, transcending religious and cultural divides to unite the people of Haiti in their shared vision for a better future.

President Martine's unwavering leadership and the collective resolve of the international coalition were instrumental in restoring peace and stability to Haiti. Strengthened law enforcement, enhanced border controls, and international support sent a clear message that criminality would no longer be tolerated, paving the way for a brighter tomorrow.

As calm settled over the nation, the leaders looked upon the changes with a sense of pride and fulfillment. The vision they had envisioned for so many years was becoming a reality before their eyes. The people of Haiti, resilient and determined, embraced the newfound peace with open arms, their spirits unshackled from the chains of fear and violence. In the corridors of diplomacy and on the streets of Port-au-Prince, the echoes of change reverberated. The international leaders, united in purpose and driven by a shared commitment to peace, had succeeded in breaking the chains that had hindered Haiti's progress for far too long. As they stood together, gazing upon the transformed landscape, they knew that their journey was far from over, but the path ahead was illuminated by the promise of a brighter tomorrow for Haiti and its people.

CHAPTER 46
THE PROMISED LAND

As the sun rose over the horizon, casting a golden glow over the streets of Port-au-Prince, the city awoke to a new dawn – a dawn of hope, resilience, and limitless possibilities. The journey chronicled in these pages had been one of trials and triumphs, challenges and victories, but above all, it had been a testament to the indomitable spirit of the Haitian people.

Annette, Marcus, Professor Sophie, Jean-Claude, Sheikh Ahmed, Bishop Ruiz, Rabbi Cohen, and President Martine stood together one last time, reflecting on the transformative journey that had brought them to this moment. They had witnessed the resilience of communities, the power of unity, and the triumph of hope over adversity.

The streets, once marred by violence and despair, were now alive with the vibrant energy of progress and renewal. Schools echoed with the laughter of children eager to learn, markets bustled with activity as entrepreneurs showcased their goods, and parks became gathering spaces for families to enjoy moments of peace and tranquility.

Economic initiatives spearheaded by Marcus and Jean-Claude had laid the foundation for sustainable growth, creating jobs, empowering communities, and fostering economic independence. The scars of the past had been replaced by the promise of a brighter future, where every citizen had the opportunity to thrive and succeed.

Through the unwavering commitment of Sheikh Ahmed, Bishop Ruiz, and Rabbi Cohen, interfaith harmony had flourished, uniting diverse communities in a shared vision of peace and cooperation. Cultural landmarks once threatened by violence stood as symbols of resilience, preserving the rich heritage of Haiti for future generations to cherish.

President Martine's steadfast leadership had guided the nation through turbulent waters, inspiring hope and instilling confidence in the hearts of the people. Her vision of a united and prosperous Haiti had become a reality, a beacon of progress that shone brightly on the world stage.

As the leaders looked out over the transformed city, they knew that their journey was far from over. Challenges would inevitably arise, and obstacles would need to be overcome, but they faced the future with renewed determination and unwavering optimism.

The book chronicling their journey – a journey of resilience, unity, and hope – would serve as a reminder of what could be achieved when people came together in pursuit of a common goal. It would inspire future generations to dream big, to never give up in the face of adversity, and to always strive for a better tomorrow.

And so, as the final chapter of their story came to a close, the leaders of Haiti stood together, united in their commitment to building a nation where peace, prosperity, and opportunity flourished. As the sun rose higher in the sky, casting its warm embrace over the city, they looked forward to the future with hope and anticipation, knowing that the best was yet to come.